Harlem Streets, 1981, oil painting on canvas by LeRoy Neiman.
Donated by the artist to Communities In Schools and used with permission.

Praise for FROM THE REARVIEW MIRROR

"Bill Milliken is a rare human being who possesses heart, wisdom, and compassion. Read <u>From the Rearview Mirror</u> and relish the goodness of this man."

— **Goldie Hawn,** entertainer and philanthropist

"Dr. Martin Luther King, Jr., spoke of the need for a dedicated circle of transformed nonconformists to offer hope to a world in crisis. Bill Milliken is one of those nonconformists who demonstrates that our small efforts to guide and invest in the next generation will pay great dividends. May we all be inspired by his life and his lessons."

— **Dr. Robert Franklin,** president, Morehouse College

"Bill has gone where the heartache is—met school dropouts on rooftops and street corners and changed the way we think about public education in this country. In this book, we see where his passion comes from and how it was shaped by failure as much as success. Inspiring, courageous, and well-written!"

— **Marjory Zoet Bankson,** author of
The Call to the Soul and *Creative Aging*

"People think of me as a hip-hop pioneer and serial entrepreneur, but I'm also someone who has worked hard for many years to integrate spiritual values and practice into my everyday world and to help others do the same. It is from this perspective that I'm delighted to recommend this wonderful book by my good friend Bill Milliken."

— **Russell Simmons,** producer, entrepreneur, and author

"Bill Milliken shares his 50-year journey of personal, professional, and spiritual challenge and triumph, loss and growth, hope and reconciliation. He also throws in a few miracles along the way. It's a fascinating story of a remarkable life, and a road map for others who want to make a difference in this world."

— **Stedman Graham,** best-selling author,
educator, and entrepreneur

"One of the extraordinary blessings I've had in my life is the unique relationship I've had with Bill Milliken. What began as a quest to solve a critical problem in American education evolved into a spiritual journey with a selfless, wise, compassionate person who guided me to <u>my</u> life's purpose. We will never know the true impact of Bill's work. Generations of families have been saved by his prescient observations of how to 'love a child to success.' We talk about one-of-a-kind people in life. He truly is <u>one of a kind.</u>"

— **Elaine Wynn,** director, Wynn Resorts, and national board chair, Communities In Schools

FROM THE
REARVIEW
MIRROR

To Randy + Paula –
I thank God for
the two of you +
for the gift of your
love + friendship –

Peace + Justice,

Bill

ALSO BY BILL MILLIKEN

TOUGH LOVE

SO LONG, SWEET JESUS

THE LAST DROPOUT: Stop the Epidemic!*

*Available from Hay House
Please visit:

Hay House USA: www.hayhouse.com®
Hay House Australia: www.hayhouse.com.au
Hay House UK: www.hayhouse.co.uk
Hay House South Africa: www.hayhouse.co.za
Hay House India: www.hayhouse.co.in

FROM THE
REARVIEW
MIRROR

Reflecting on Connecting the Dots

BILL MILLIKEN

HAY HOUSE, INC.
Carlsbad, California • New York City
London • Sydney • Johannesburg
Vancouver • Hong Kong • New Delhi

Published and distributed in the United States by: Hay House, Inc.: www.hayhouse.
com® • *Published and distributed in Australia by:* Hay House Australia Pty. Ltd.: www.
hayhouse.com.au • *Published and distributed in the United Kingdom by:* Hay House
UK, Ltd.: www.hayhouse.co.uk • *Published and distributed in the Republic of South
Africa by:* Hay House SA (Pty), Ltd.: www.hayhouse.co.za • *Distributed in Canada by:*
Raincoast: www.raincoast.com • *Published in India by:* Hay House Publishers India:
www.hayhouse.co.in

Cover design: Charles McStravick • *Interior design:* Tricia Breidenthal

Library of Congress Cataloging-in-Publication Data

Milliken, Bill.
 From the rearview mirror : reflecting on connecting the dots / Bill
Milliken.
    p. cm.
 ISBN 978-1-4019-3790-4 (pbk.)
 1. Milliken, Bill. 2. Communities In Schools
(Organization)--Biography. 3. Youth workers--United States--Biography.
4. Community and school--United States. 5. Dropouts--United
States--Prevention. I. Title.
 LC221.M552 2012
 370.92--dc23
 [B]
                              2011049423

Tradepaper ISBN: 978-1-4019-3790-4
Hardcover ISBN: 978-1-4019-4133-8
Digital ISBN: 978-1-4019-3791-1

15 14 13 12 4 3 2 1
1st edition, June 2012

To my brother Bob—thanks for never giving up on me.

CONTENTS

"You can't connect the dots looking forward; you can only connect them looking backwards. So you have to trust that the dots will somehow connect in your future. You have to trust in something— your gut, destiny, life, karma, whatever. This approach has never let me down, and it has made all the difference in my life."

— STEVE JOBS

"Finding the treasure is only the beginning of the search."

— FATHER HENRI J. M. NOUWEN

FOREWORD

by Cory Booker, mayor of Newark, New Jersey

The book you're about to read is the story of a life lived with energy, faith, and openness to change and growth. It's a story about answering life's highest calling to serve. It's truly an extraordinary journey.

I first met Bill Milliken shortly after I was elected mayor of Newark, when he came to our city in his role as founder of Communities In Schools (CIS), which has a strong presence in Newark. CIS is helping thousands of young men and women throughout our nation to get the education they need and the future they deserve. Meeting Bill was an experience. I was immediately struck by his humility, by the kindness that seemed to be so thorough and authentic. He was a man of great accomplishment, but he had a youthful wonder about him, a light that seemed to emanate from his core and a sense of peace and hope that was infectious. The organization that he founded immediately made more sense to me; it was in many ways a natural outgrowth of the man. Communities In Schools is, in a sense, his values and spirit made manifest.

This is the power of Bill's book: *From the Rearview Mirror* shows how a person's outward journey reflects the inward path as well. What we see outside ourselves in the society that surrounds us—despair or hope, dead ends or possibilities—is a reflection of who we are inside. From a young age, Bill was forced to confront the challenges of growing up as a "different learner" (or "dumb," as he was called back then). As a result, he had to choose: Would he live a life of possibilities, committing to his potential and helping others recognize theirs, or would he surrender to his fears and self-doubts?

It's Bill's struggle, his conscious choices, and his determination not to let the world shape his spirit but instead have his spirit shape the world that offer the rest of us powerful lessons in service and love. Perhaps serving others begins with recognizing your own worth, abilities, and truth. Bill demonstrates that this recognition of self opens up the ability to see the truth of others and to serve and love them unconditionally.

This is something I rejoice in about Bill—he doesn't get caught up in a cult of personality. When you sit with him and talk about Communities In Schools, it's not about him and his accomplishments. His humility is a force that calls us to understand what we can do and accomplish together. Bill was once told by a prospective funder that only "charismatic and unusually dedicated people" can change the world. I love it that he doesn't believe this. If we wait for such individuals, nothing will change—and worse, we'll fail to see the great leadership that abounds around us.

This is the model that has made Communities In Schools so successful—a deep and abiding faith that we aren't ordinary. Instead, we have extraordinary potential; and our schools, children, and neighborhoods abound with far greater hope and possibilities than we readily realize.

I'm grateful Bill has chosen to write this story. These pages are filled with his spirit, and in reading them we can discover more of our own truth. What Bill Milliken sees in his rearview mirror is a road map for our future—a future I believe is abundant with hope.

INTRODUCTION

A Letter to My Grandchildren

Dear Alexandra and Jack:

Yes, I decided to write another book. I know you're probably thinking, *Now Pops is in really big trouble. He's always telling us he's read three books in his entire life, and also written three. So he'll have to figure out how to pick a fourth book to read.* I promise I'll somehow get through one more before this is in print—or at least before you finish high school, Alex. It will be a pretty thin book, I imagine.

I've been reluctant to do more writing because I'm not all that interested in memoirs, and I wasn't sure I had anything new to say. But now I realize that I do. I've reached the fourth quarter of life, and as I look into the rearview mirror, back six decades or more, I can see and understand so much more about the journey than I did while I was living it. I believe there are insights that I can pass on to others, including a new generation that's energized to fight for social justice.

As you probably know, I'm one of those people who "learn differently," and so is your Aunt Lani, your Dad's sister. We don't see things in a linear fashion. I always knew I had a relational mind, and I could make connections among incidents and ideas that weren't always obvious to others. When I try to put words on paper, that's the way I think and write. Sometimes it gets messy! So this book doesn't always follow a strict chronological order as I chase down the memories and insights that shaped my life.

I've also been thinking that *everyone* who's reached that fourth quarter of life has his or her own story that needs to be told, now more than ever. The world you're growing up in is more and more connected—and is less and less a community. All this technology is helping us learn more about things than we ever imagined, and about one another, but without knowing the person. We have lots of interesting and often helpful "informationships"—as I call these new, technology-based ways of connecting—but they can't substitute for one-on-one personal relationships.

The two of you have been blessed not only with incredibly loving parents, but also by being surrounded by adoring grandparents who live within shouting distance. Add to that your wonderful extended family of uncles, aunts, and cousins, and you have what I call a community of caring adults and a safe place to learn and grow—two of the Five Basics I've championed through Communities In Schools, the organization I helped found. As you grow older, you'll discover that many of the people you meet on your journey haven't been as blessed as the two of you. As for me, without the love and help of countless people who stood by me over the years, I could never have made it.

The world you and I now live in is "smaller" and more a part of the global community. It's also growing increasingly divided between those who have resources and those who don't. This era is filled with so much uncertainty. You're being raised at a time of great economic instability, a time of wars and threats of terrorism, of great danger to our planet and environment. These are all issues that have no boundaries and no quick solutions. So many of your peers are growing up with overfed bodies, underfed minds, and starving souls.

As you become more aware of this world around you, it may be easy to fall into despair, especially with all the noise of our airwaves, blogs, and tweets sending messages of doom and gloom. I urge you and your friends not to buy into such defeatism and doubt, or fall into the trap of escapism.

Was I born with this outlook? No, I wasn't—that's very clear in the rearview mirror. You probably look at your Pops now and think, *Gee, he seems pretty happy. He looks like he's got it together. Lots of people love him, and he loves them back.* But it took me many years to feel safe and accepted, to find a place I could call my own.

Your Pops moved into Harlem in 1960 at the age of 20, spending from 1960 to 1971 there and on the Lower East Side of Manhattan. This, too, was a time of uncertainty and fear. Our country was engaged in a very unpopular war in Vietnam, and millions of us found ourselves on the streets protesting. During a number of those years, I had up to 35 young people living with me who had no homes or places to stay. A dozen of them didn't make it—they either were shot or overdosed on drugs.

I was very angry during that period and in much despair. I felt caught between the privileged community I'd grown up in and the tragic realities of the community I'd chosen to join. I couldn't believe that there were so many young people without hope or a future just blocks from some of the wealthiest individuals on Earth. I wanted to bring this broken nation together, make it whole, "with liberty and justice for all." And although I didn't realize it then, I wanted to heal myself, too, to find a family and a community I could truly belong to.

At that time in our nation's story, there was much social unrest over civil rights for African American citizens. We saw regular footage on our TV screens of people being beaten and jailed simply because they wanted the equality and justice that was promised by the founders of our country. And in the midst of this, we saw three of our leaders assassinated, men who were national heroes—President John F. Kennedy; his brother Robert, who was a senator and candidate for President; and the Reverend Dr. Martin Luther King, Jr., our national leader in the fight for civil rights.

So those were difficult and uncertain times of change, just like now. It was easy to fall into despair, to long to escape from it all, or to get so angry that no one wanted to be around you. Your grandmother and I would never have imagined that we'd see an African American President, a Hispanic Supreme Court justice, or a female secretary of state or speaker of the house.

Also, I never thought I'd see the day when our campuses are again full of young people who are motivated to do so much to give back to their communities, who not only want to do well in their vocations, but also want to do good for their neighbors. And finally, in a time of intense political division, we see people coming together across political lines around one burning issue: the need to ensure that *all* children have an equal chance in life, starting with a great education. That is the same issue that your grandfather and his colleagues have been working on all these years. Back in the '60s, I never thought I'd see the day come when we have a chance to really turn around our failing public schools.

And if I'm being honest with you, I never thought I'd be alive in 2012—alive, happy, and whole, with the family I always wanted. Somehow God healed my brokenness, and that, too, is part of the story told in these pages.

Jack and Alex, it's an amazing thing to be alive. You won't really understand your journey until someday you look into the rearview mirror of recollection and experience, just as I'm doing in this book—but that's all right. There's plenty to understand right here, right now.

One final request: Do Pops a favor. If anyone asks about this crazy grandfather on the Milliken side, and they don't have time to read the book, here are the four main insights that have guided me in writing it:

- Life, while often confusing and painful, is also incredibly good, a never-ending journey from hurting to hope to healing. This is the power of love in action.

- The theme of my life journey has been *connecting the dots*, trying to bring together the fragmented communities that I feared I could never belong to. In the process, I found and confronted my own brokenness.

- My spiritual journey—my own personal walk with God—has faced many of the issues and challenges of modern believers, and I think it demonstrates that even a flawed and sometimes bewildered pilgrim can find a way to put spiritual principles into practice.

- I've lived and struggled during a time in American history that has left an enduring legacy of social consciousness, service to others, collective change, and commitment to social justice. This book is my best shot at passing on some hard-won wisdom, lessons, life experiences, and insights to the next generation.

I hope the two of you enjoy this book one day. I pray it will make your own journeys just a little easier and more blessed.

Much love,
Pops

CHAPTER ONE

I'M NOT GOING TO MAKE IT WITHOUT YOU

Vinnie De Pasquale and I had been waiting for this day for many months. It was June 17, 1960, and we were about to move into a two-room tenement apartment at 117th Street and Lenox Avenue in Harlem, New York. Vinnie had recently gotten out of jail, and I'd just finished the second of what would be my three freshman years of college.

I was 20 years old and about to start a journey that would take me from Harlem and the Lower East Side to the centers of power in Washington, D.C., from a street mission to a national movement—a journey that has shown me that *life is about relationships and grace.*

We were in Harlem to try to do something unique. As members of a youth organization called Young Life, we wanted to reach out to the poorest and most neglected members of society. Our qualifications to do this consisted of exactly one thing: a mutual gift for hanging out. I'm still lobbying to get schools to give a degree in that.

Our friend and mentor Harv Oostdyk was the head of Young Life in New Jersey. I'd met him and Vinnie at a Young Life youth camp in Colorado, but I never dreamed we'd end up on the streets of Harlem together.

The apartment cost $32 a month. It had one bedroom, into which we managed to squeeze two beds. The bathtub was in the kitchen, and there was no hot water. Nor was there any escape from the intense summer heat—air conditioning was the impossible dream in a flat like this one. That first night, sweating in our airless bedroom, we could smell garbage out in the alley and hear a constant scurrying that was either roaches or rats—most likely both.

In the morning, we set our plan in motion. Not much of a plan, but for two guys with a "major" in hanging out, it was all we needed. We grabbed a basketball and walked to the nearest park, looking for a court and some kids we could get a game with.

We had no trouble finding the kids. The park was full of street youth, hard-core drug users and dropouts, most of them either home-less or unwilling to go home. They seemed to be anywhere from 15 to their early 20s, standing around smoking and talking, drinking beer, or playing some serious ball on the beat-up blacktop court. They stared at us, not saying a word.

What did they see? There was Vinnie, a few years older than I was, a former Golden Gloves boxer, a recovered heroin addict, an ex-con with tattoos all over his body, wearing dark sunglasses and looking very "street" himself. And there was me: If Vinnie looked street, I looked the opposite. I was a fresh-faced suburban kid, a Little Lord Fauntleroy who kept grinning at everybody and saying, "Hey, wanna play basketball?" And just to complete the joke, I couldn't play. The only dribbling I did was on my chin, and you could maybe fit a piece of paper underneath my feet when I went for my jump shot, but I was willing to pass a lot and toss the ball up there when I could.

In short, these kids saw two white idiots trying to get into their game. I didn't figure this out at the time, but what saved our asses was that these street-smart youth immediately drew the obvious con-clusion: we were cops, and very lame cops at that. Two white guys, one tough and one "nice," walk up and start acting friendly? What else could we be? So instead of beating the shit out of us, they pretended we weren't there. They knew better than to take out a cop.

That's my memory of our first attempt to hang out in Harlem. And it probably describes pretty well the next several days, too. After hours of hostile looks and rejection, Vinnie and I would go back to our stifling apartment. We'd have a sandwich for dinner, drink a lot of water, and hit the sack as soon as it got dark. The minute we turned out the lights, out came the cockroaches—they sounded like an army coming to haul us away, mattresses and all.

"Yeah," Vinnie said, "and they're so big, and this place is so small, they're probably hunchbacked roaches."

The next morning, we'd be back at the park. I'd walk up to a guy on a park bench, and he'd move away to avoid me. If I tried to shake hands, the guy would look away. If I attempted to join a group for basketball, everyone else got chosen before me—which was actually pretty sensible!

I can't pretend it didn't hurt, though. It brought up a lot of childhood pain, feelings I'd carried with me for a long time about not fitting in, not being accepted. This silent rejection was worse than overt hostility, because if somebody yelled at me or gave me a hard time, at least there was interaction, dialogue—something could happen. This way, all my fine ideas about "street work" just went down the drain, leaving me feeling like a failure.

But finally, Vinnie started to get in some games, since he could actually play. We began learning the names of the young people, talking to them between games, telling them why we were there. A lot of the kids still thought we were cops—probably narcs, since we didn't seem to be investigating any particular crime—but then the word got around that Vinnie and I *lived* in Harlem. As far as I know, no narc in New York City had ever done that (this was long before "community policing"). So, strange as it seemed, it looked as though we might be on the level, and slowly some of these young men started to believe what we were telling them.

So what *were* we telling them? What did we think we could offer them? To explain that, I need to talk about what happened to me when I was 17 and first met Vinnie and Harv.

It was 1957, and I was just about living at Nobbie's Pool Hall in Wilkinsburg, a suburb of Pittsburgh, with a bunch of other "losers" called the Green Street Animals. A child of the 1940s and '50s, I was brought up in an affluent middle-class neighborhood; my father owned a successful brick factory and drove a Mercedes; we had the country club at our disposal.

Yet by the time I was 17, I'd left high school. I had no hopes, no future. I was involved in petty crime and had little to no relationship with my parents. One day, an older guy named Bob started hanging around at the pool hall, trying to overcome our suspicion and get to know us. It turned out he was a Young Life youth worker, and he wanted to start a club for kids in our neighborhood.

I wasn't interested in that, but when he invited me and five of my pool-hall buddies to spend a week at a Young Life camp in Colorado, we signed up. Frontier Ranch was located at the base of Mount Princeton, southwest of Colorado Springs. It was the most beautiful place I'd ever seen. The scenery was incredible, there were horses and swimming pools, and everybody was friendly. There was even a free pool hall. And yes, there were girls I could impress with my street cool. Young people from all over the country came to Frontier Ranch each summer, brought by various Young Life counselors who were doing the same kind of outreach work that Bob had done with me and my friends. (Harv Oostdyk wasn't there that first summer. I met him and Vinnie and some of their friends from the streets of Newark on my next trip to the ranch, the following year.)

Then one evening we had a big meeting for all the campers—which I went into feeling hostile because it was starting to remind me of school—and some adult I'd never seen before stood up and starting talking about God and Christ. What a crock! I could hardly admit it to myself, but part of me had been feeling excited about this camp. I'd been sensing some new possibilities, and I was so longing for community, for people to see me and welcome me. Now here was the hidden agenda . . . religion. I'd been conned.

When I attended church with my parents, it was obvious that Christians were complete hypocrites as far as I could see. Not that you could really blame them, because wasn't the whole God thing crazy?

Why would God care about people? Why would he care about *me?* I was a loser.

When the meeting ended, I went looking for Bob, and when I found him, I called him every name I could think of. I accused him of lying to me, of deliberately concealing what Young Life was about.

Bob didn't try to weasel out of it. He looked me in the eye and said, "You wouldn't have come if you'd known what it was, right?"

"You're damn right I wouldn't have."

"Well, I apologize for tricking you, but I'm not sorry that you're here."

Angry as I was, I respected him for leveling with me, and I could tell he respected me, too, and wasn't trying to bullshit me.

"Bill, I think you're prejudiced," Bob went on. "You have a preconception of who God is. I challenge you to listen and consider what's being said about him here. You might find it's the most important thing you've ever heard. And if not, then just enjoy the camp, and no hard feelings."

I was too confused to reply, so I turned my back on him and walked away.

I SURPRISED MYSELF, THOUGH. I was able to put aside my resentments and do what Bob had suggested—just enjoy the camp even if I didn't want to hear anything about a spiritual life. There was something going on every hour of the day. We rode horses, climbed mountains, put on skits, and had a lot of time to talk to the camp counselors and each other.

I was learning perhaps the most important lesson of my life—not just my life *then*, but for the next 50 years as well. *Personal relationships are the key to change.* No program in the world is going to help a young person find his future. And sermons, proselytizing, and guilt trips aren't going to open anyone up to the Spirit. I needed to find adults I could trust and who trusted me. I needed a reason to hope. Bob and the other counselors saw *exactly* who I was—an angry, ignorant, unhappy young man—and they loved me anyway. The Young Life people were for real. They loved me unconditionally, whether I believed in God or not. There were no strings attached.

Never in my life had anyone related to me that way. My parents should have given me unconditional love—but they hadn't. My teachers kept wanting me to be someone I wasn't. Even the Green Street Animals would have dropped me like a shot if I'd stopped being tough and "cool." This Colorado experience was a first.

One of the people I liked the best at camp was the cook, Andrew "Goldbrick" Delaney. He and his wife, Jerry, had been feeding hungry kids at Young Life camps since they first began. He was a warm, good-humored man, always there for me, always concerned about how I was doing.

Jerry, on the other hand, could be a little . . . difficult. She had a notoriously short temper, especially around her kitchen. It became a (somewhat dangerous) game for us campers to see if we could rile her up. One time, I was in the process of disorganizing the kitchen and generally bugging her when she picked up a meat cleaver and started toward me. Would she have used it? I guess not, but I didn't want to take any chances. I ran out and dove into the swimming pool until she calmed down.

There was another thing about Goldbrick and Jerry: they were African American. In fact, they were the only blacks at the ranch. It raised some uncomfortable memories and questions for me. Back in Wilkinsburg, I'd become aware of the rigid racial and social divides of my community (which I'll talk about more later on). Here in Colorado, everyone treated the Delaneys with respect and affection. There wasn't a trace of prejudice. But . . . why *were* they the only African Americans there? Why were all the campers white? Even in 1957, I had a strong feeling that this was going to change—it *had* to, especially if all the "Jesus stuff" I was hearing had any validity.

So I didn't immediately start trusting Bob, Goldbrick, or anyone else. I liked them all, but there's a big difference between liking and trusting, and it all came to a head one morning.

Frontier Ranch had work crews as well as fun activities because the counselors wanted us to experience the satisfaction of collaborating on a job well done. We were filling holes in a dirt road, and I was slacking off.

Bob called me on it. "You're lazy!" he said.

I threw a shovelful of dirt in his face, and then I took off running down the road.

I don't know where I thought I was going. We were out in the middle of nowhere, at least two hours from Denver. I just knew that I had to leave before I got thrown out. What I'd done was completely against the rules of the camp, and part of what I was coming to respect about the Young Life leaders was that they meant what they said. They were true to their word. Yes, it was tough love—and this is where I first learned the concept. So I knew they weren't going to make any exceptions for me after I'd done a ridiculous and spiteful thing like that.

I probably didn't get too far down the road away from the ranch, although it felt like miles, and I was miserable and angry inside. Then I heard a jeep pulling up behind me. It was Goldbrick Delaney. He'd seen me taking off, and he'd come to stop me.

"Come on," he said. "Come back to my cabin with me. Tell me what happened."

I went with him and told him the tale. He looked grave; he knew it was a very serious situation. But he said he'd talk to Jim Rayburn, the founder of Young Life, who was there at the camp, and see if I might be allowed to stay on the condition that I'd seek out Bob, own my bad behavior, and ask for his forgiveness.

I stayed in Goldbrick's cabin while the staff had a special meeting about the incident. Finally, Goldbrick came back and told me that Bob was willing to hear what I had to say. So together we went and found Bob, and I apologized. He accepted my apology and made some wisecrack to lighten the atmosphere. I found that I respected him even more. This was a man who walked his talk. He'd told me that he believed in forgiveness, and now he was living that principle.

So the staff told me they'd try to stick it out with me. Once again, I saw that personal relationships meant more to these folks than anything else—more than rules, more than discipline. They actually cared about *me* and wanted me to have another chance. As long as I was honest about my behavior and my feelings, their love was inexhaustible.

EACH NIGHT AT CAMP, WE HAD what the counselors called a "roundup" in an old wooden auditorium. This was where the talk would turn to God, and of course my friends and I would sit in the back and goof off. But as the week went on, I started listening more and more. The whole atmosphere of the place was designed to make us curious. I wasn't good at school, but I was always very open, always probing and wanting to know more. So I asked a lot of questions and listened carefully to the answers. That was my way of learning.

The Young Life leaders challenged me intellectually to give up my preconceived notions of God. They didn't talk doctrine and tell me what to believe. Instead, they told stories, using metaphors from Scripture. Young Life's motto was: "It's a sin to bore a kid," and they really brought the whole thing alive for me.

In a small way, I began to see that the God that Bob and the others were talking about was totally different from my own experiences or ideas—the stuff I thought I knew from church. This wasn't about "clouds of judgment," or a stern Lord with no time for someone like me. They were talking about an incarnated God who cared, who walked with us, and about how we were created in his image.

They spoke of the price of love. "There's a real cost to following Christ," Bob said. This wasn't sentimental, the nice Hollywood-movie "I love you" kind of thing. It was sacrificial, a love that gives everything. That really appealed to my all-or-nothing personality. Anything I've ever done, good or bad, I've done 100 percent.

So even though I remained doubtful and skeptical, I wanted to believe what they were talking about. That someone would care about *me*, with all my screwups—it really was "good news," if only it were true.

On the final night, we all gathered for the roundup. Jim told us that God cared so much about us that he sent his own son to live and suffer and walk through the valley of the shadow of death with us. God wanted to dwell with us and in us. He was knocking on the door of our lives. We could have a relationship with this God right now. This wasn't an intellectual challenge anymore—this was a call to action.

I didn't let on to my friends, but I was really moved. Afterward, we spilled out of the auditorium into the cool Colorado night where a big bonfire was crackling. The counselors called us to gather around the fire and said, "If any of you discovered God this week, ask God to take over your life."

I was blown away that a lot of kids did stand up and talk about what had happened to them. I just stayed in the back and didn't say anything. But before the meeting broke up, I walked off into the darkness, away from the others, with the bright full moon lighting my way. At the foot of Mount Princeton, I stopped.

"God," I said, "I don't know if you're real, but I need this very much. I'm not going to make it without you. If you can take someone who isn't sure about you but is hungry for meaning and hope, then please enter my life." The tears were rolling down my face, and suddenly, something happened. It's hard to explain exactly what. I felt a calm, a peace I'd never known before. It was mysterious and real; I knew I wasn't making it up.

When I returned, I told Bob about it, but I asked him not to tell everybody else and make a big example of me. I was still a little skeptical of the people who stood up and "gave their lives to Jesus" in public. To me, it was very personal. Besides, I had my reputation to protect, so I didn't go around talking about it.

But privately, I decided I was betting my whole life on this. I had nothing to lose. And I also had no idea how radical and difficult this kind of love is, no idea what an incredible journey I was about to embark upon. I didn't become another person all at once. It was a beginning, an opening up. I knew I'd never be the same again, and I was right. This was the start of a process that has never stopped. The transformation is still at work as I enter my 70s.

In every age and every culture, people have had personal encounters with God that changed their lives. This was mine. But please don't imagine I went from lost to found in one week. Maybe that happened to Saint Paul, but it sure didn't happen to me. If it had, there'd be no need for me to write this book.

So WHEN VINNIE AND I—BOTH OF US committed members of Young Life by this point—started to hang out in Harlem, we were trying to do for others the same thing that had been done for us. Someone had cared about us, valued us, and loved us unconditionally. They felt we were worth something. They wanted us to have a spiritual life. We wanted to share this with the youth we met on the streets.

Was this naïve? To this day, I don't think so. Sure, it took longer than we thought it would to be accepted and trusted. But once that happened, our basic beliefs about personal relationships were confirmed. The minute young people realized that we cared about *them*, wanted to know *them*, wanted to be there for *them*, they reacted just the way I'd responded to Bob and the other Young Life counselors.

Vinnie and I began to build relationships with a number of kids who desperately wanted a better way of life and were willing to consider making a spiritual change for the better. We tried many different ways to connect with them and quickly figured out that fun, physical activities worked best. A lot of these young men had skipped the enjoyable parts of childhood.

For that matter, I was only a couple of years older than some of them myself. I couldn't tell the difference between us sometimes. I didn't know how to be "the adult" and didn't really want to—I wanted to have fun, too.

Vinnie and I got some used mattresses, and we'd throw them down in the park or at a church gym and teach wrestling. I'd gone out for the sport in high school and during the first of my three freshman years in college. My nickname was "Canvasback," which wasn't good, since it meant I spent a lot of time on my back looking up at the ceiling. But I learned the moves and could teach them.

My first pupil, I remember, was a guy called Snake. He was 20 pounds heavier than I was, a little shorter but a lot stockier. He was all muscle. Snake didn't quite get the rules at first. He picked me up, bear-hugged me, then slammed me to the floor, missing the mattress and knocking me out. He felt bad about it, though, and it actually helped to build our relationship.

So-called tough kids need a chance to show caring and concern. A year or two later, when we took some New York street guys out to the Colorado ranch, we were riding horses when my horse tripped and rolled over, and I got knocked out. When I came to, they were all gathered around me, their faces full of fear. Up until then, they'd been sort of hard and not into sharing their feelings. Now they had an excuse to show they cared about me.

Anyway, I wouldn't recommend either of these ways to build relationships—much too hard on the skull.

Vinnie and I took the guys on day trips to Coney Island, to the amusement park and the beach. A lot of these kids had never seen the ocean, never been out of their housing project. This was a way to do stuff with no resources. We'd just ride the subway or get in a beat-up van and head to New Jersey, where Harv Oostdyk's father had a barn. We'd go on overnight trips there and see some nature. We hiked, played touch football—anything to get them to experience life outside of their little world.

The streets could be exciting at times, but a life of tenements, subways, and housing projects, full of violence and poverty, is so limited and dangerous. We wanted them to become curious about what else was out there, just as I did when I went to the Colorado camp.

There were opportunities to talk on these trips, but we never pressed anyone. If a young person was interested in knowing about us, what we were all about, then we'd tell him. Building relationships always came first.

ON THE PRACTICAL SIDE, THE WAY IT WORKED back then was that Young Life would officially sponsor someone to do street work and eventually start a new club. But part of the arrangement was that the person in question had to raise funds to pay all his own expenses—including money to live on. So right from the start, we had to make connections with local churches and other nonprofit, youth-serving groups who might be willing to donate space, goods, and hopefully a little cash.

Our work got considerably easier when Dr. Eugene Callender offered us a base of operations at his Church of the Master on Morningside Avenue, within walking distance of our apartment. Dr. Callender had been hearing a lot about us—most of it positive, fortunately—and made a pretty bold decision to support these young white guys.

The Church of the Master was one of the oldest and most renowned African American congregations in Harlem, with a reputation for activism and outreach to the often-struggling community. There was an indoor basketball court and a place where we could start a regular Young Life club, with weekly meetings to help young people get on course and have some fun along the way.

Before very many months passed, though, we came to a tough realization: our new friends needed more than a club and more than a spiritual path. I remember Vinnie saying it perfectly: "How can we claim to love our neighbors and let them sleep in alleyways? We go out there and tell them how much we care, and then we leave them without a roof over their heads."

What was missing was *community*. Somehow we had to find a way to create a community for young people that would offer them the basics—food, shelter, safety, and education—without which, frankly, it's pretty hard to care much about your spiritual life.

And man, did that ever press some buttons inside me. I knew it wasn't just about community for *them*. All my life, I'd been longing for the same thing. Once again, let me go back and focus on my upbringing in Pittsburgh. It will explain a lot about what happened in New York over the next ten years.

BEING RAISED IN A MIDDLE-CLASS SUBURBAN FAMILY gives you a lot of advantages—and puts a lot of pressure on you as well. My parents expected me to behave myself and do well in school. And through third grade, I was a good kid, a good student. But then it all changed, and looking back, I know it must have had a lot to do with the way I learned—or *didn't* learn.

I understand now that I learn differently from others. My brain doesn't "imprint" words in the typical way. So when was I reading in school, it just didn't sink in. I literally couldn't make sense of it and wouldn't remember what I'd just seen on the page.

One learning specialist I talked to as an adult called it "disappearing ink," and that's exactly what it feels like. To this day, if I'm giving a speech and I look down at my notes, it can interrupt my flow completely because I'm suddenly switching into a different mode of cognition. And sometimes I remember that awful phrase that *every* kid like me thinks: *If they only knew. . . .* It felt as if I were constantly covering up a terrible secret, and any minute someone could come along and expose it.

No one was informed about that stuff back then, though. It wasn't called "learning differently." Teachers just thought I was dumb and uncooperative, and my parents weren't involved enough to set them straight—if they even knew. I was one of those hyperactive, wisecracking kids who couldn't sit still and pay attention. And even when I told the truth, it sounded like I was smarting off.

Once, my fourth-grade teacher, Mrs. Grundy, made me come up to the front of the class and read. Then she asked me to talk about what the passage meant. I was humiliated and embarrassed.

I said, "I can't remember what I read," which was absolutely true, but she assumed I was trying to be funny.

"You weren't raised right," she scolded me.

"Well, you weren't raised right either," I retorted.

Once again, I was on my way to the principal's office to learn more about the back side of my lap. Paddling was a legitimate part of the school experience back then.

Somehow I kept getting promoted, but I have no doubt it was what we call social promotion today. The school just didn't know what to do with me. And frankly, I was a good hustler. My verbal skills were always strong. I was already starting to develop some alternative abilities that would help me find my place and my calling.

I had the family credentials to belong to the upper middle class. As I said, my father owned a brick company, and the Millikens were country-club members. I looked as though I could fit in anywhere, but inside I didn't feel it, and in fact it wasn't true. I couldn't find anything in common with children from my neighborhood, and I couldn't keep up with them in school.

My only friend from near where I lived was a kid named Frankie. He was a small, slight guy like me who got teased a lot, so I didn't feel as if we were competing. We walked home from school together, and sometimes we'd play at his house, where his parents had polka music on the record player all the time. (I guess they were Polish, or maybe they just liked to polka.) I didn't feel inferior to Frankie—in fact, I felt a little protective of him and tried to defend him from some of the bigger kids.

Then one day I saw an ambulance pull up in front his house. After years of constant bullying, Frankie had gone home from school and hanged himself. He was maybe 11 or so.

Whatever I felt about that, I pushed it way down inside. No one talked to me about Frankie or asked me how I was doing. But I'm pretty sure his suicide planted a seed that later grew into a powerful conviction: *There's no excuse for turning your back on a defenseless child. Every kid needs someone to care about him.*

MOST OF THE OTHER KIDS WERE BIGGER than I was, and I lost a lot of fights. One guy, Sammy Tedesco, was a *lot* bigger. One day when I was in the sixth grade, I got cornered in the boys' room by a bunch of tough kids. I lost it and started fighting back like an animal. Sammy, for some reason, was the one I chose to vent all my anger on. They had to pull me off him—I was pushing his face into the urinal.

But from that day on, Sammy never disrespected me again. Instead, he befriended me and started inviting me over to his house. We were equals now. I was accepted, and from then on, Sammy was the one I always got in trouble with. Something about him clicked with my own rebelliousness and alienation. Teachers didn't give "time outs" in those days; they gave time off, so we wound up hanging around at the janitor's office in the boiler room when we were tossed out of class. (In fact, that gave me a lifelong appreciation of how important the janitor is in the school community.) I can still see and smell that boiler room. It's a good memory, because I liked the janitor and I liked not being in class.

Going over to Sammy's was amazing for me. He lived in a slightly more affluent neighborhood near ours. Everyone in Wilkinsburg knew the rumors about his family's mob connections. "Fingers" Tedesco, Sammy's father, earned his name from being an expert safecracker. He was also a bootlegger, a numbers runner, and the best chess player I ever met—no one could beat him. He had a great mathematical mind and a great criminal mind. Sammy had inherited the same abilities, except his game was checkers. I loved hanging out with his family. They accepted me, they fed me, and they welcomed me.

When we were teenagers, I went on some of Sammy's numbers runs. A lot of people today may not know what "playing the numbers" meant 50 years ago. It was like the lottery, except it was illegal. People laid down bets on what particular number would come up each day. For example, sometimes it might be the last three figures in the daily attendance at a Pittsburgh Pirates game. It didn't matter; it could be anything, as long as it was obviously on the up-and-up.

The winners collected pretty big, maybe a couple of thousand dollars. They'd get a predetermined percentage of all the bets, and the numbers guys would pocket the rest. Sammy would go around the community, showing up at various shops and street corners, taking the bets for his father. He wrote it all up in a big book—cash only.

It may sound harmless, but these were mob guys; and if you crossed them, you got hurt. I saw Sammy break people's legs when they tried to muscle in on the Tedesco territory. And although I never saw it, I know people got killed, too.

As for my parents, the best way I can put it is that they had a hard time raising kids. My brothers, Bob and Ken, were a lot older than I was, and they were out of the house by the time I entered my mid-teens. I think I was more like a pet than a son to my folks.

My dad was very distant. It was the era when fathers weren't necessarily expected to be into "parenting," but he was extreme even for that time. It was just the way my family was. When he died in the 1970s, I wasn't there—I was on a plane heading home because nobody had told me he was sick until it was too late. He died while I was in mid-air. Despite his distance, he was lovable, gentle, and quiet. He supported himself through Penn State by playing piano with the swing band known as Fred Waring and His Pennsylvanians.

I did have my father's example in one way. He'd worked hard to build up the family business, and he placed a high value on that. I know I embarrassed him with my stealing and con games, but he had no idea what to do about it.

My mother was ill through most of the time I was growing up. Alcoholism and emotional problems, serious physical illnesses that required surgery . . . it was very tough for her. She could be charming when she was sober, but then it would all change. One time when she was drunk, she yelled at me and told me that she hadn't wanted any more children after Bob and Ken, and that if she had to have a third child, she wished I'd been a girl. It wounded me deeply, but then Mom was verbally abusive to all of us. It was always the alcohol talking, but it still hurt a lot. My oldest brother Bob and I both had similar experiences. We can remember happy moments growing up, but our mother was never in the picture for most of them.

I couldn't deal with her drinking. Once, when I was 16, I heard a sound from the kitchen. I knew what it was: the top of a liquor bottle being unscrewed. My mother was supposed to be on the wagon, so I charged in and confronted her, and in a matter of minutes I found 18 bottles hidden all over the house. I smashed every one, walked out, and thumbed my way to Camden, New Jersey. A guy named Stump Jackson, a friend of Sammy's, lived there, and he let me crash at his apartment. But I could only stand it for a week before I was ready to go back home. Stump's hoodlum colleagues were giving me funny looks, as though I had no business being there, and the neighborhood felt totally unsafe. I was just a kid, and these were grown-up criminals.

Children of alcoholics tend to become addicts themselves, or else they never want to go near a bottle. My brother Ken—good-looking, charismatic, and a millionaire by the time he was 23—took the first route. He made a fortune buying and selling real estate (what came to be called "flipping houses"), but the disease cost him his career. His wife took their three children and walked out on him, and he eventually got mixed up with gangsters who beat him within an inch of his life.

One time when I was in my 20s, I got a call from one of Ken's friends, telling me that my brother was in bad trouble. I went back to Pittsburgh and found Ken in a flophouse. I had to break down the door because he kept insisting that he was fine and didn't need any help. I couldn't believe what he looked like when I finally got inside the tiny room. He was literally yellow, and his liver was so distended that he looked like he was pregnant.

You'd think that would be a bad enough bottom for any drunk. But nothing changed for Ken, and he wouldn't speak to me for years afterward because I'd "interfered" with his life choices. Ken survived until he was 69, when his alcoholism finally killed him.

Bob and I went the other way, choosing near abstinence from alcohol and staying completely away from any other drug. That instinctive decision was incredibly fortunate for me, considering all the trouble I got into anyway. If I'd been drinking and drugging, too, I'm sure I wouldn't be alive today.

Basically, the way I was raised gave me the advantage of no structure. I was free to do what I wanted, and it made me creative and energetic. And that was also the *disadvantage* of no structure, because "what I wanted" was usually bad for me. I had no boundaries. Years later, when I was living in New York City and providing safe places for street kids, I had to face this issue all over again. I was great at hugging, loving, and supporting them, but I had no clue how to provide structure or discipline.

My creativity came out in all kinds of ways, most of them involving misbehavior. When I was 13, I organized a BB-gun brigade. Behind our suburb was a wooded, hilly area where we had encounters with the enemy—kids who lived in the next neighborhood down the hill and who were a little more well-to-do. I proposed the terms of engagement: Instead of throwing stones, we'd use BB guns, but the rule was, no shooting above the knees. (It didn't always work out that way.) There were fewer of us, but we won way more battles than we lost because I learned how to outflank our opponents. At sunset, they'd be coming up the hill with the sun in their eyes, and they always let themselves get out-positioned, never catching on. So I definitely had strategic skills. I also had three BBs in my right leg, just below the kneecap—I have them still.

A little later, I started a shoplifting ring. There was nothing very original here. Some of us would talk to the clerk up front while the others lifted stuff, mostly cigarettes and Spam. We hid the loot in some old tires behind my parents' garage until my father discovered it. This didn't break up the ring; I just learned not to be stupid enough to hide contraband around the house.

Every now and then, my childhood creativity hit a positive note. One time I organized the younger kids into a cherry business. A number of yards in our neighborhood had cherry trees, and I got the kids to pick the fruit and bottle them. Then I did a survey of which homes didn't have the trees, and the kids would knock on the doors and sell the cherries. People were more likely to buy from cute little kids, whom I let have 75 percent of the profits. I didn't do any picking; I was the mastermind, the entrepreneur.

When I hung out with Sammy and the other "hoods" our own age, it was a continuation of my rebellious creativity, and it also felt like community. We would do stupid stuff, mostly—stealing cigarettes to resell, cornering the market on various desirable goods in the neighborhood—but some of it was violent and dangerous, too. I got in a number of serious fights, and my nose has been broken five times, three of them from those teenage rumbles. Yet I don't want to give the impression that I was tough. It was all an act—especially compared to guys like Sammy. It was my version of the act that every young person puts on in order to cover up hurt and vulnerability.

MY SEARCH FOR COMMUNITY TOOK ME in another direction as well. The hill where we lived was for whites only, of course. All the successful families, including us Millikens, were Republicans. Irish and Italian immigrants (like the Tedescos) were grudgingly allowed in, but they were never considered equals. They were Catholic, for one thing, and having Catholic friends wasn't the thing to do. It was made clear to me that my father's family was Scotch-Irish and English and definitely Protestant.

Down near the football stadium, a few African American families started to move in, attracted by the steel industry that was flourishing after the war. If one or two black kids showed up at my school, that was fine, as long as they kept their place, helped the basketball team, and never complained. It was a perfect illustration of racist, segregated America in the '40s and '50s. There was no busing, no integration. Blacks and whites walked separate, unequal paths.

The only African American I actually knew personally as a child was Thelma, a wonderful woman who took care of my mother. Because my mother was sick so much, I spent a lot of time with Thelma at our house and also at hers. When she was done with her workday, she'd let me tag along back to her home. She lived quite close to us, but it was another world. Everything depended on where you lived—on the hill or down below. I walked to school, and I could walk another ten minutes and be at her place.

Thelma lived in a row house with her extended family, children, and grandchildren. My brother Bob is almost ten years older than I am, and he remembers coming home to visit and realizing that I was virtually living over at Thelma's. He could see that things had gotten a lot worse at home. Years later he told me, "I remember you as such a sweet, sweet kid. My little brother! And then I saw you get really badly hurt."

Throughout my middle-school years, I depended on Thelma for all the love and acceptance I craved. We never talked about it, but I'm sure she was a person of faith. Her relationship with God shone through everything she did.

She also taught me to dance, and I can still see my father at the piano, playing one of his old Fats Waller standards while Thelma showed me how to boogie. I was probably about 13, which would have been around the time my mother was so critically ill that the pastor came and anointed her in preparation for death. She pulled through that time, but looking back, I understand how important Thelma was to our sad household. My father was unable to express his feelings (although music brought out a joy in him like nothing else), so Thelma gave me all the warmth she could.

I recall sitting on her porch one day, looking out at the street and at her family hanging around with me. And it dawned on me: *I'm the only white face here. This is a whole other world only ten minutes from my house.* It was an important moment for a sheltered middle-class white kid, although I know it doesn't sound like much. I never forgot it—that sense of how close their lives were to mine, yet how great a distance stood between us.

I'VE TALKED A LOT ABOUT ALL THE WAYS I didn't fit in, all my problems with family, school, and community. But any time I wanted to show up at the country club, the door was open to me. I was one of the Millikens, respected leaders in the Wilkinsburg business world. Even in school, where I was constantly faking it in class, a lot of my peers trusted and liked me. I realized I had a strong, genuine desire to get to know people, to build relationships with them. But I was already starting to hang out at Nobbie's Pool Hall, and the guys I met there were the only ones I really felt comfortable with.

My big moment of high-school success came when a bunch of my companions from Nobbie's nominated me for class vice president without bothering to tell me. Basically, this position's only duty was to organize the prom. Of course it was a joke from their point of view: "You look straight, and you've got a crew cut, so let's get you elected and you can run the prom."

They told me what they'd done and asked, "So will you campaign?" I said, "Hell no!"

They campaigned for me anyway, and I got elected. Although I didn't want to admit it, there was this feeling inside: *I'm accepted.* Besides, I discovered the prom committee was all girls, so when they asked, "Will you serve?" I said, "Hell yes!"

Sometimes it nearly drove me crazy, the constant feeling of being stuck between worlds, of not fitting in anyplace. I had no idea who I was and no idea how to find out. You can't imagine how badly I wanted a close, nurturing community. . . .

FOUR YEARS LATER, I WAS DISCOVERING that the youth in our Harlem Young Life club needed the same thing. I was being called to create a community for me and for them that would demonstrate whether my "love" was for real or just talk.

I now know that life offers us these precious opportunities—the grace—to heal our own wounds in our interactions with others. I couldn't have put it that way in 1960, but I felt the deep calling of community and knew that I had to respond.

We were soon given a practical way to do so. Dr. Callender at Church of the Master had connections with Trinity parish, a big

Episcopal church on Wall Street. One of their missions was called St. Christopher's Chapel, and through the chapel's generosity, we could receive free rent at a brownstone house full of apartments at 215 Madison Street on the Lower East Side. Harv Oostdyk and Vinnie stayed in Harlem to continue working with the youth there, and in September I moved downtown to create a live-in community at 215 Madison for as many young people as I could persuade to try it.

It was my first experience with "replication," a concept that would challenge and often frustrate me throughout my journey over the following decades. I wanted to take what I was learning in Harlem and do it again, only better. Fortunately, I still had Harv and Vinnie as colleagues. We stayed in close touch, and all three of us felt that we were working different aspects of the same mission, the same calling.

Still, I needed a new apartment mate, someone who was willing to offer a huge amount of help with this challenge. Through God's grace, I joined forces with a great guy from Young Life named Dean Borgman, an ex-paratrooper from Connecticut. (I'll talk more about Dean shortly—he was such an important mentor for me.) I had a feeling that the Lower East Side was going to prove an even tougher environment than Harlem. But I knew without question that this was the right path for me, because I could feel so strongly how the inward and outward journeys were starting to weave together.

The rest of my story is about that interweaving. It's about how hurting can lead to hope, and how hope leads to healing. Most of all, it's about how a young guy from suburban Pittsburgh found grace and love that transformed his own life, even as he tried to transform the lives of others. It's about community, and how I finally found mine.

CHAPTER TWO

LEARNING TOUGH LOVE

My friend Bo Nixon grew up in a completely different world from mine. It was the realm I was about to enter—the dangerous, divided streets of New York's Lower East Side in 1960.

"I grew up hating," Bo wrote in a magazine article years later. "Everything I saw around me was broken. Broken bottles littered the alleys . . . Winos hung out on the corners . . . Mothers cried over their junkie sons. And mine was a broken home."

Robert "Bobo" Nixon and his mother and siblings lived in the Alfred E. Smith Housing Project, which consisted of 12 buildings, with 17 floors per building. Bo's father left the family when he was very young. His mother tried her hardest to raise six children, but often the best Bo could expect was a whipping for making bad decisions.

He grew up full of anger, especially toward white people. A grade-school teacher (I guess she was his Mrs. Grundy) once accused him of stealing a pen that belonged to the teacher's pet. When Bo denied it, the teacher said, "It's bad enough to steal, but lying is worse," then took Bo's pen away from him and gave it to the other kid, who was white, as was the teacher.

Bo was crying when his mother came home. She told him to forget about it and said, "There's nothing you can do about some things in this life."

But Bo discovered there *was* something he could do. At 13, he joined one of the most violent gangs on the Lower East Side. When I met him he was the fearsome president of the Centurions, commanding 150 soldiers. He was 18 years old.

I was hanging out one hot Indian-summer afternoon at a basketball court near the projects, watching a pickup game. Up walked Bo with a few of his inner circle. He was eyeing me—I obviously stood out. I already knew who he was. He'd been pointed out to me from my first day in the neighborhood. Bo's gang controlled the streets from the Brooklyn Bridge to the Williamsburg Bridge at the end of Lower Manhattan, which was the big divide. Beyond that, the Sportsmen controlled everything. Bo was their number one enemy.

Bo was a little shorter than I was, very dark skinned and muscular, with piercing eyes that observed all that was going on around him. When he looked at you, those eyes gazed right through you.

Standing there by the basketball court as he approached, I felt my stomach tie itself up in knots. All I could do was what I always did: I went up to him and said, "Wanna play basketball?"

Bo made it clear—using language that's too rough even for me— that he'd prefer to kick my ass all the way back to Pittsburgh. He walked off, followed by his henchmen, and the whole court breathed a sigh. This guy had such power, so much leadership and strength. From that day, I knew that if I could somehow reach Bo Nixon, things would begin to turn for us on the Lower East Side.

Our new home at 215 Madison Street reminded me a lot of my old flat in Harlem. It had the same stifling, cramped quarters and the same cold water—even the roaches and rats looked familiar. Maybe they'd followed me down from 117th Street. The difference was that Dean and I were living in a building divided into five apartments, and our goal was to create a community in that building where street youth, most of whom had dropped out of school and were struggling with drugs and gangs, could find a safe place to begin turning their lives around.

I mentioned that Dean was an ex-paratrooper. Other than that, he and I had a lot in common. Like me, he'd hung around with a bunch of suburban kids in trouble with the law both before and after his tour of duty. Eventually he got tired of people hassling him about his future.

"What am I supposed to tell 'em?" he asked. "'I plan to hang out with kids for the rest of my life'?"

So he came to New York to work toward a doctorate on the GI Bill, then began teaching high school and taking classes at Columbia University. He also became firmly committed to Young Life and its mission to reach out to urban youth.

Dean taught me so much. He was older than I was and really brilliant, and he called things like they were. He and Harv, my other mentor, were both innovators. They could set boundaries and schedules even in the most challenging environments. Dean was always saying, "We've got to create some order in this place!"

When it came to relating to kids, Dean was more the traditional father, and I was the mother, although sometimes we switched roles. My approach was warm and encouraging, but it also tended to create chaos because I didn't know anything about boundaries and was trying too hard to be nice.

There was a guy called Wolf whom we were thinking of offering a place to live at 215 Madison. We invited him over for a talk in order to get to know him better, and it went very smoothly. We were impressed with Wolf and decided to let him move in. Then after he left, Dean grabbed me and pointed into the back room, where we'd been doing some repairs.

"Damn! He walked out with our electric drill!" Dean exclaimed.

I played my usual nice-guy role and countered, "How do you know? We don't know it was him. How did he get a drill out of here?"

"I *know* it was him," Dean said. "He's the only one who's been here, and that drill went out under his jacket. He's going to pawn it."

I said, "Okay, let's confront him."

So we got him back over, and Dean took the heavy hand, very stern. Wolf reacted by calling him a motherfucker and stalking out.

I followed him and said, "Hey, all you have to do is admit it. And bring it back." We ended up taking a long walk together, and I kept saying, "We really want you to move in. Dean's being tough here, but he understands, and so do I. Let's make a new start."

And Wolf did admit it, returned the drill, and lived at 215 Madison for quite a while. It was the combination of both Dean's and my approaches that made things work. I always started out wanting to make excuses and give everyone the benefit of the doubt, while Dean wanted to get in their face. He showed me that discipline was a type of caring. We came to call it "tough love," and it became the guiding principle in our new community-building work on the Lower East Side and the title of my first book.

IN CONTRAST TO HARLEM, THIS NEIGHBORHOOD was a clearly defined patchwork, demarcated by racial and ethnic boundaries. On one side of our apartment house were the Italians. On the other side were the blacks and Hispanics in the Smith housing project, and a huge Chinese area was right next to that. Everyone stayed within their own turf. As Bo puts it, "If they got out of place, we had a few riots of our own!"

This was the gang era, too, and there were always explosions. Guns were less common, but some of the gang members had them, and there were plenty of fatal stabbings during the constant battling. Bo remembers how the social agencies, churches, and police got together to try to stop the violence in the community. This was what Dean and I walked into.

"You were very naïve," Bo tells me. "I guess you were learning on the job."

Our first few days on the Lower East Side felt like a replay of my introduction to Harlem. We walked the streets hour after hour, and when we got tired of walking, we sat on the benches in the park with the guys or hung out at the basketball courts. Clark Jones, another local teen who'd soon become my lifelong friend (and years later, along with his wife, Edith, godparent to my daughter, Lani), says that once again, everyone thought we were cops. He adds, "I also thought you were just plain stupid. I thought you were in a place where you didn't belong."

Every night, Dean and I went back to the smelly gloom of the tenement. We'd lie in the dark, wondering if we'd always be outsiders. Yet I felt strongly that I was where I was supposed to be. At least I was hanging out with a purpose instead of throwing my life away. Dean would nod and sigh. Then we'd hear the rats start crawling up through a hole behind the toilet. Honestly, I was more scared of the vermin than the hostile street kids. And the rats weren't scared of anything—they came in swarms from the docks, as big as horses, it seemed like.

Dean invited his younger brother Dave to join us at 215 Madison a couple of weeks later. And it was Dave who first made the connection with Clark Jones, who also lived in the Smith housing projects but hadn't joined a gang. Unlike so many of the young people we'd meet, Clark had a strong family, and his father wouldn't let him. He didn't drink or smoke pot, either. "I didn't feel I had anything to prove," is how he puts it.

Clark was respected by, and got along with, everyone in the projects—gang members included. There were a few incidents where he was challenged or ridiculed for not being a soldier, but there was a limit to the criticism, because everyone knew Clark Jones was good with his hands and wasn't afraid to use them. You didn't want to push him too far.

So when Dave encountered him on the basketball court, Clark was willing to shoot some hoops. Slowly, some friends of Clark's started to hang around with the crazy white guys, too. Up until that point, the only experience these street kids had with integration was between blacks and Hispanics, because they went to school together. But outside of school, they knew exactly where the boundaries were.

Most of the time, the only dialogue they ever had with white guys was: "Don't come over here!" So our presence was confusing. They could see that we had resources, interests, and concerns; and we in turn could see that they were curious about us, even welcoming.

When we started planning our trip back to the Colorado ranch in the summer of 1961, Clark was the first kid we approached.

"When I was first asked to go on the camping trip," he recalls, "and was told it was in Colorado, I said, 'Where's Colorado?' I didn't know much geography, right? I knew where the Bronx was."

But Clark said he'd ask his parents—which, believe me, was a very unusual thing—and he came back and told us he'd go. We didn't want him to be the only black youth on the bus, so we asked him to choose a friend to come along, and Tom Moore joined him.

Our trips to Colorado became annual events for the next several years, and sometimes it's hard for me to sort out the memories of which incident happened when. But overall, these were some of the most challenging and rewarding experiences I ever had.

We'd load up the rickety old bus with as many as 40 kids. The first several years, there were only a few blacks, as Young Life was recruiting kids from all over the East Coast, not just urban areas. The inner-city youth—my guys—were leaving New York for the first time in their lives and mixing with white kids their own age who weren't trying to beat them up. The differences were both positive and negative.

"I was on the bus with these white, upper-middle-class kids," says Clark. "They had money, man! They'd be spending $20, $30 every stop. I had like $20 for the whole week."

Within a year or two, we had a whole busload of guys from Harlem and the Lower East Side going to camp every summer. I'd look down the aisle of the bus, and there were Manny Perez, Wolf, Snake, Butch Rodriguez—all these gang kids and drug users—and I knew some of them were still packing, so I always brought along an old empty barrel.

I'd wait until we were halfway across the country and it was good and dark out, and then I'd tell them, "If I catch any of you with drugs or knives or guns on this bus, I'm going to stop and leave you in the middle of a cornfield." Then I'd put the barrel at the front of the bus.

None of these guys had ever been outside the five boroughs, and I knew they were terrified of being stuck there among the scarecrows, with not a city light in sight. I'd stay up while everyone was supposed to be asleep as we drove through the night, and soon there came soft footsteps, and I'd hear *clink, clink, clank* . . .

We had to drive straight through to Colorado because at that time in history, with the civil rights movement still gaining momentum, you didn't want to stop a bus full of African American teenagers in a whites-only community. One time we varied from that routine, and it nearly got us killed.

Our air conditioning had broken, and we were melting on that bus somewhere in Kansas—it must have been 100 degrees, no breeze, just constant sweating. We drove into a little town around sunup and saw some college-age kids cleaning a public pool. Everyone started clamoring to go swimming: "We gotta cool off, man!" I was dying of the heat, too, so I said that I'd see what I could do.

I went up to the pool attendants and said, "Hey, how about if I give you a few bucks, and you let these kids have a swim before the pool opens." They said okay—I was white, and they had no idea that the "kids" would be black—and I signaled for everyone to pile out and dive in. About 30 minutes later, we were splashing around and feeling great when we heard this rattling sound from the chain-link fence around the pool. What seemed like a battalion of whites was pressed up against the fence, shaking it to get our attention. Then we heard, "*Niggers, niggers . . .*"

Next came the sheriff and his people: "Get these boys out of here, right now."

I knew this was no place to stage a civil-rights protest—besides, it was obvious we needed an escort. We rushed back onto the bus and were followed to the town limits by that cop car. The sheriff made it very clear he never wanted to see us in his town again.

As we drove off down the two-lane highway, the kids were pretty quiet—in fact, they stayed quiet for the rest of the trip to Colorado. Before the swimming-pool episode, there'd been the usual bickering and tension between the various cliques. But this had unified everybody; they were survivors. I could also tell that most of them were terrified by what had happened, but of course they couldn't show it and keep their street cred.

I had surprisingly little trouble from the guys on any of the bus trips. I guess they really wanted to check out the camp, so they were willing to temporarily give up their bad habits. In the ten years I took kids to Colorado, I only had to kick out one person, whom I caught with a switchblade. I took him to the nearest Greyhound station and said, "Do what you have to do to get home, but you're not going to camp." He threatened to get me, but when we got home, the other guys watched out for me.

I WOULD HAVE BEEN A LOT MORE SCARED if that last incident had involved a guy like Bo Nixon. He was no one to mess with. Bo had been suspicious of me the entire time I hung out in the park playing basketball, and I knew he didn't trust me enough to come out to the camp.

It was Harlem all over again: "Who is this white guy? Motherfucker lives right in the neighborhood with two other guys, so he's probably not a narc, but . . ."

The white kids stayed in one park; the blacks stayed in another. So when I deliberately came to their park, Bo couldn't figure my angle. Still, I was able to win some of his friends over just by knowing their names, coming around every day, and hanging out.

Much to Bo's disgust, his younger brother Tap agreed to go to Colorado in the summer of 1962. He came back and told Bo, "You ought to give these guys a chance. The sales pitch is all true. We had a great time."

All Tap wanted to do was play ball. (And eventually he played basketball for Long Beach State in California, then became the head of the Department of Recreation in Long Beach.) Bo was different, much more serious and respected.

During these first trips to Colorado, a number of kids had a similar experience to mine—they heard the good news that God personally cared about them, and they understood God's love through the staff and the atmosphere of the camp. Clark and Tap, in particular, wanted to stay on this new path. They told me, "We need a support group on the streets. It was nice up there on the mountain, but we're back in the 'valley' now."

Their commitment was sincere, but they knew they weren't going to make it without help. And they were leaning on me, a person who was in some ways just as screwed up as they were.

In response, we started a Young Life club and also a group called the Cross Carriers (12 guys, modeled after Christ's disciples), which offered some simple rules for living: no bars, no drugs, no fighting, mutual support, and spiritual guidance. We also began taking in young people to live with us in the apartments at 215 Madison, kids who had no place to go and wanted to get off the streets.

The word was out that even guys who'd been involved in violence, theft, and drugs would be accepted in our community. They knew we stood for a different world, a square world. They knew we didn't approve of their negative values. But they also knew that we cared about them anyway. Once again, it showed the incredible power of simply loving people unconditionally and telling them that you believe they're valuable, that they have something to give.

I HAD ANOTHER ADVANTAGE WHEN I STARTED to build one-on-one relationships with the Lower East Side youth. To a man, they'd dropped out of school and were convinced they were "losers" by society's standards. That was exactly my own experience. Those early, humiliating incidents where I learned to call myself "dumb" never got any better. I'd managed to stay in school up until I was 17, bluffing my way through, but the day came when that all changed.

The principal called my mother into a meeting and told her that she ought to withdraw me. I was getting into way too much trouble, he said. I was hanging around with a bad crowd (if only he knew the half of it!), wasting my time down at Nobbie's Pool Hall. And besides, I couldn't handle the schoolwork.

That was the phrase he used: "Bill can't handle the work." I knew exactly what that meant: I was dumb. I was so stupid that I couldn't even finish high school.

"Fine," I told my parents. "Take me out of school."

It was actually a big relief. I could spend my days in the one place I felt real and honest. The principal had been right on target about Nobbie's—I spent all my time there. I felt there was more communication, more community, in that scruffy room with its six pool tables, bar, and smoky haze than I found anywhere else. I talked the way I liked to, and nobody rejected me for it. I had credibility; I had an identity. It was yet another "family," just like the Tedescos, just like Thelma's house.

It was also the continuation of a dangerous, dead-end pattern for me. My friends and I lived day to day with no higher purpose, no goals, and no plans. I remember well how the time just dragged on and on. I used to lie in bed at night in tears, wondering where I was headed and what my life was really about.

This is what my first 17 years imprinted on me: *You don't fit. You're stuck in the middle, stuck between worlds. You're not happy with your family, you're not happy in school, and—if you're honest about it—you're not really happy at Nobbie's either. There just isn't any place for someone like you.*

So when I moved to New York as a young adult, and my new friends on the Lower East Side opened up and talked about how lost and useless they felt, they were singing my song. There I was, still try-ing to find a place where I belonged, where I had value. But at least my experience of isolation made it easier to understand and relate to them.

SOMETIMES 215 MADISON FELT LIKE Grand Central Station. People were constantly coming around to talk, hang out, and be safe. Dean felt that we were a kind of extended family, a place where an individu-al could struggle through some of the emotional development he hadn't been able to do at home. You can bet that rang some bells with me—I knew *exactly* what that felt like.

Each person had to maintain himself, and that helped build re-sponsibility and self-respect. Everyone was equal; everyone was encouraged to share food and clothing and activities together. St. Christopher's Chapel invited us over every night for the evening meal, so that was another chance to learn social skills and feel like a part of something.

Sometimes this backfired, though, like the time Johnny B. left the dinner early to head back to 215 Madison. He was new to our community and just off heroin. We all went back about 15 minutes later and began our house meeting, but there was no Johnny B.

Dean asked, "Anybody seen him?"

A guy named Armando said, "Oh yeah, I saw him going down the steps."

I was looking around and noticed our TV was gone. When I pointed this out, Armando said, "Oh yeah, I saw him carrying the TV down the steps." He'd left out that little detail. Dean and I both glared at him and after a second he added, "And I think it was him who took the refrigerator, too."

We'd been scratching our heads over that missing fridge for a week. It could be a funny story—except Johnny B. was back on the streets and back on the needle, and we never saw him again.

It may sound as if we were constantly getting ripped off. That's because we were. At least it helped us practice spiritual values such as sharing and not getting attached to material things. We didn't have much stuff to begin with, and what little we had was often heading out the door.

There were house rules: Attend the daily meeting. No stealing drills, TVs, and refrigerators! Keep your room clean (interpretations of this varied widely). No physical violence.

We had one basic rule that mattered most, and it was a hard one: You have to be honest. The only surefire destroyer of community is lying. We told everyone, "We don't care what you've done in the past or right now, but you have to tell the truth about it." This was the bedrock of our "tough love" idea, and it cost us many young people. We had to *mean* it: If you lie, you're out—no excuses.

One of the worst moments occurred when Manny Perez, a young man we'd been through a lot with, refused to talk to us about whether he was getting high. Manny was one of my favorites, a real leader and very intelligent. But I knew how hard he was struggling with drugs. One night, we came back to 215 Madison from our communal supper at the parish hall and gathered for the house meeting, where everyone could speak his mind and hash out whatever issues were brewing.

I was sure Manny was using smack. When I asked him straight out, he said nothing, just looked at the floor. The other guys told him to level with us, but he just sat there. So we all took a vote and told him, "If you're willing to get honest with us, you stay. If you won't, you go."

It was a horrible decision to have to make, but Dean and I knew that as soon as we allowed anyone to break the honesty rule, there quickly wouldn't be any rules left at all. This time I had to reverse roles and stay tough. "Mothering" wasn't going to work.

Manny suddenly exploded, calling me every name in the book. Then he threw his apartment keys at me.

"Okay, where do you want to go?" I asked.

He said that he had an uncle in Brooklyn. It was late and pouring rain, so I said I'd drive him.

As we crossed the Brooklyn Bridge, Manny suddenly reached over from the passenger seat, yanked up the emergency brake, and shouted, "Let me out here!" He got out and jumped over a low railing. He was on a narrow ledge, three feet from the edge of the bridge.

I felt sick. "Manny, what are you going to do?"

"I don't know. Maybe I'll jump off this fucking bridge." He started walking up the ledge and vanished in the darkness.

For three months, no one knew what had happened to him. Then we got word on the street that he was still alive. Soon we heard a little more: The Army had told him that if he could stay clean for one year, he could come back and enlist. It sounded like he had a plan, which he'd never had before in all the time he was living with us.

I never heard from Manny again—until almost 40 years later. After I gave a speech in Newark, New Jersey, I walked out and headed for the train station. There was a guy standing there in the darkness. My survival instincts kicked in, and I was ready to run, but then he called my name. It was Manny.

He told me that he'd seen an article in the paper announcing that I was scheduled to talk, and he came down from Elizabeth, New Jersey, because he wanted to thank me. He said that as much as he appreciated my caring and support during his first years at 215 Madison, we were basically enabling him. It wasn't until we showed him the tough side of love along with compassion and really held him accountable for his actions that he was able to reach inside himself and decide what he wanted to do.

ONE THING THAT'S BOTHERED ME OVER THE YEARS is the way the phrase *tough love* has been misused by a lot of different people since I published my book of that title in 1968. It's fine for others to adopt the concept, but not when it's used to mean an uncompassionate, kick-ass sort of attitude. We never meant it that way. For us, it was about accountability. When we told Manny, "The only thing you can't do is lie," it was for his own good and for the benefit of everyone in the apartments. Breaking trust is the hardest thing to get past because it damages community so badly.

It's very easy to tell other people, "Oh yes, use tough love." I learned that the things we come on strong about, the things we're always recommending to others, are usually our hidden fears and weaknesses. The truth is that I've always found it very hard to practice tough love. I tend to wait till the tension builds up, which is perfectly natural. Anyone who tells you that they *like* confrontation . . . well, they need some help!

I saw so much conflict and violence on the Lower East Side that I often just wanted to get away from it. It was constant and frightening. The last thing I wanted to do was go home at night and then practice tough love with a young person I was living with. But I had to learn what confrontation really means.

It's an emotionally draining, difficult way to show your love in action. You have to give people their freedom, and that sometimes means living with the consequences of their choices. You have to let go and let God be in charge. Continuing to "help" them isn't always helpful. It can prevent them from hitting bottom and finding solid ground to build their life on from there.

The important thing for me is the word *love*. It's not punitive, and it's not busting someone's chops. It says, "Because I really care about you, I'm going to tell you what I see; and you can say it back and tell me if I'm accurate." And the other person knows it's hard for you to say that. He doesn't have to agree with you, but he has to know that he's been heard and that he's heard you, all straight up and no dodging around. Then it doesn't escalate until the anger gets out of hand and becomes violent and inappropriate. And the choices are clear.

The most common—and most damaging—issue at 215 Madison was drugs. When a kid got high, we didn't throw him out, but our standards were explicit. The continued use of drugs would put guys out of the apartment eventually. It was understood that there could be one, two, or even more failures, which they'd have to admit clearly and talk over with us. There'd be warnings, but as soon as we sensed that they were giving in to failure in any way, they were put out.

It was one of the hardest things I've ever had to do. It's easy when you can put your arm around a guy and say, "You're wonderful." But telling a kid, "Okay, it's time you grew up and accepted responsibility. I don't want to hear any more excuses" is hard, especially when you know how horrible that kid's options are. But nothing else worked. Time and time again, we had to say, "I don't care how this makes you feel toward me. You may hate my guts, but I love you, and I'm doing this *because* I love you. I don't expect you'll understand right now, but I have to do it anyway."

The pain of addiction I experienced in my family was a big part of why I was always so down on drug use. My wife, Jean, later said that when she first knew me, I was the only person she'd ever met who didn't drink or smoke. I was always the designated driver because everyone around me drank all the time. Our country's attitude about alcohol has come a long way in the last 50 years, and that's great news. People still drink—a lot—but no one thinks drunk driving is funny anymore, and there's vastly more information and support for treating alcoholism. It's so clear: addiction is addiction is addiction, no matter whether the drug is legal or not.

BUT MY FAMILY'S PAIN OVER ALCOHOLISM wasn't the only reason I was anti-drug. When I moved into New York City, heroin was everywhere—what Claude Brown, in *Manchild in the Promised Land*, called "the shit plague." It seemed like half the guys on the street were strung out, using heroin to stop the pain of their dead-end lives. The drug was such a powerful force. We all knew about the guy later portrayed in the movie *American Gangster,* but he was like a spirit—we heard about him, but no one ever met him. He lived in Jersey in a nice house. It didn't take me long to conclude that the number one thing that could bring down this country was drugs. I still feel that way.

Oddly enough, at that time one of the few forces *against* drug use was the gangs. If you were in Bo's gang and used drugs, you'd get thrown out.

"We didn't want any part of it," Bo says. "We saw what had happened to a lot of the older guys who'd been in the gang and then got into drugs. We'd see them on the corner, nodding off. They were in and out of jail. We didn't want that for ourselves."

So Dean, Dave, and I were often faced with a situation where we'd persuade some kid to leave a gang, only to watch him get strung out on heroin.

I wasn't afraid of much, but I had two of the most terrifying nights of my life staying up with guys getting off drugs cold turkey. It did make me start thinking about demons. They were seeing stuff I sure wasn't, shivering and cursing, wrapped up in blankets and calling me a motherfucker. A couple of other guys sat outside the door so the addicts couldn't get out. There were no fancy rehabs back then, at least not for poor people. There wasn't even Narcotics Anonymous because New York State had very punitive drug laws that made it a crime for addicts to meet together for any reason, including trying to stay clean. If you wanted to kick drugs, you did it on your own.

Putting addicts in prison has never done any good. I saw what happened when they were incarcerated: they went from being day laborers to learning how to run the business. Dwight Kellogg, an ex-con I knew back then, used to tell me, "Man, when I needed some drugs, I had to get arrested—they were much more available in prison."

It's not just poor minority kids who turn to drugs, although people who ought to know better still believe that. One time, I got a call from the ex-wife of a wealthy Wall Street executive, pleading with me to help their son kick heroin. She and her husband were two of the richest people on the East Coast, and she knew me because they'd both been great supporters of our work on the streets.

So I met her son and watched him go through hell, trying to get clean. But then he'd always be right back out on the street. It was obvious what the problem was.

I told his mother, "You're going to kill your son. Every time I get him back on his feet, you or your ex-husband give him money."

Nobody had ever talked to her like that, and I knew it might mean I'd lose her future support, but I had no choice but to be clear.

"If you keep giving him money," I said, "he's going to be dead. He may die anyway because he's so addicted, but if you keep on enabling him, I guarantee it."

This particular story had a happy ending: her son got clean and stayed clean, finally. He's a successful man today, and I'm thankful his life was spared. I went to so many funerals of kids I cared about, promising young lives ended in an alleyway with a needle in their arm.

ALL THIS TIME, TRYING TO BUILD OUR COMMUNITY at 215 Madison, I kept my eye on Bo Nixon. I knew Tap and Clark had given him a good report about the Colorado camp. When the summer of the third trip rolled around, I approached him again about going with us, and this time he said yes.

So, like other inner-city youth before and after him, Bo was exposed to parts of the country he'd never seen before and met white people who were loving and interested in what he was all about. It was so different for him because there was simply no place to have conversations like that back in the neighborhood.

I told Bo, "You don't have to do anything at camp if you don't want to, except for one thing—you have to come to the evening meetings." So he'd stand in the back and kind of watch the other kids. They sat on the floor, but Bo wouldn't. They were singing! Bo Nixon, the leader of the Centurions, sitting around and singing religious songs with kids? No way. So he'd just observe, and then there'd be a speaker. We'd have discussion time at night in the cabin, and I tried to raise questions about what we'd heard.

At the end of that camp experience, something finally loosened up inside Bo, and he decided to find a way to follow Christ. Like me, he was very quiet about his personal life, and he didn't make a big public thing out of his conversion. He considered it deeply private.

But when we got back to the Lower East Side, the difference in Bo became obvious. He started walking down the streets with me—literally walking his talk of brotherhood. You can't imagine how courageous it was for him to do that, and it gave me so much more credibility. Bo was so suspicious of white people, yet there he was, walking side by side with me for everyone to see. It was his vote of confidence that I had no ulterior motives, and it helped me win over a lot of others.

Still, it took a while for Bo and me to trust each other. His rage against white people hadn't gone away, and I had a number of naïve misconceptions about what I had to offer him. At first I felt afraid of him, but that had to be overcome. I saw that he had a wealth of knowledge, he was smart, and he wanted to learn. By the time he was a teenager, he'd already fought battles that most of us don't have to face until our adult years, and maybe not even then.

I came to understand that Bo and I were the same inside. When I talked about loneliness, I found he was lonely in the same way. His fear and insecurity were just like mine. When we finally connected, it was through our shared pain. We both knew what it was like to go through life hurting and angry.

Even his initial experience at Frontier Ranch was a lot like mine. I've said that I was distrustful of the counselors, especially when I found out they wanted me to learn more about God. But actually, it was more than that. I can see it plainly now, when I adjust that rearview mirror a little: I was full of rage, and I acted it out.

Of course, Bo had to deal with an aspect of the Colorado camp that, for me, merely raised curious questions: race. Growing up, he'd taken it for granted that everything worthwhile had been done by white people. That was part of his hatred. But by the time I met him, he'd learned better. A young African American social worker had given him information about some people named Frederick Douglass, George Washington Carver, and Harriet Tubman.

Bo once got in my face and asked, "Did you know that the first doctor to operate successfully on the human heart was a black man from Chicago?" I had to tell him that no, nobody ever told me that.

And there he was at a camp where black faces were still hard to find. Sure, there were Goldbrick and Jerry Delaney and a few other urban youth, but it looked pretty feeble in his eyes, and I can't blame him. Sometimes it's hard to remember what America was like in 1963. When Young Life decided to reach out to African Americans, they got swamped with protests. Some Southern clubs wouldn't let their kids go to an integrated camp.

Bo saw all this, but by God's grace he was able to transcend it. He wanted what all of us want—respect, community, safety, a chance to show he was a leader. He wanted to belong to something bigger, something that deserved his loyalty and commitment. Like most urban African Americans, he'd grown up going to church every Sunday, but he stopped when he got involved with the Centurions.

"Church attendance was no longer acceptable to my gang. And besides, I never could see how going to church helped me. Church was nothing but a bunch of people who looked nice on Sundays, and I couldn't see where it changed them. They ripped people off during the week just like everyone else," he said.

That awareness of hypocrisy was often linked in the minds of black youth to an accurate assessment of white racism. The great comedian and social activist Dick Gregory used to hang out in the Avenue D projects near where we lived. He waxed eloquent while sitting on a bench on hot summer nights.

"Oh yes," he'd say, "it's a remarkable thing those Christian missionaries did. It makes me want to become one. They gave people a Bible and took their gold and their land in return. That Jesus is just amazing!" You had to laugh because he was really nailing some truth there.

In fact, my understanding of how "following Christ" connects with—and too often is in conflict with—institutional Christianity has evolved a lot in the years since then. What I'd say now is this: I think there's a strong tendency for well-meaning believers to wind up worshipping their church instead of God, although that's not always the institution's fault. They get so caught in the rules and regulations, the dos and don'ts, of being a Presbyterian, Baptist, or Catholic that they forget what the real Christian message is. Obeying the rules and judging those who don't is an invitation to pride and condemnation of others. I sometimes feel that if there's a personal devil the way there's a personal God, then he sometimes hides behind the name of Jesus, tempting people to evil in the name of good.

Bo WAS STILL PRESIDENT OF THE CENTURIONS when he came back from the Colorado trip, so you can imagine what a big change he had to go through in trying to get out of that. I would always say to him, "You're a natural leader. Why don't you do something positive with it?" My idea was to see him literally turned around so that instead of getting kids in trouble, he'd be helping them.

It was amazing to watch him do this. Bo made peace with the gang that his soldiers fought every year, but that was just a start. He also had to work on his own temper—which he's still doing today! It was a big turning point, realizing that his language had to change and that he had to defuse the way he exploded at people.

We challenged all the guys to confront each other about whatever behavior was holding them back. Some kids were gambling, some were drinking, and some were whoring around. Bo's issue was his temper. But after a while, I pulled him aside one morning and said, "Man, you're changing. I haven't heard you blow up at anybody in a long time." He hadn't even realized it.

A few months after Bo began his turnaround, Dean and Dave Borgman and I realized that we needed help at 215 Madison. We just had too many kids to supervise, and we needed trustworthy "counselors" to live in the apartments with the new guys. So we asked Bo if he'd be willing to move out of his mom's house and into an apartment with three kids on the first floor of 215 Madison.

It turned into a kind of "each one teach one" routine. I'd go over some sort of life-skills lesson with Bo on Monday, and on Tuesday he'd teach the same thing to the kids in his apartment. The whole thing was improvised and hands-on. We were all learning what it means to be a leader and trying to model what a real Christian might look like, as we understood it. Bo and the others didn't see too much of that in their neighborhood, and I sure hadn't where I grew up. We saw a lot of people go to church, but that's not the same as seeing them try to emulate Jesus.

Once Bo moved in, Dean, Dave, and I had a different status in the neighborhood and in the apartments. Up until then, kids would use their hands on us pretty frequently, although of course it was against the house rules. If someone took a swing at me, I have to admit that I didn't always turn the other cheek. Self-defense was necessary, and a couple of times I couldn't take care of myself on the street. Some guys in the park did a real number on me once. But Bo made the difference—nobody was going to mess with us and bring down his fury on them. I eventually got a little car, and it was never broken into or stolen. I didn't fully realize how much I was protected till years later when Bo shared a few stories with me.

IT PROBABLY SOUNDS AS THOUGH I was doing good and feeling good about my calling. That's one side of the truth. The other side is that I was always afraid of being embarrassed, threatened, and seen as inadequate and dumb. Scripture says that "perfect love casts out fear," so obviously I wasn't there yet. My love still needed to get tougher.

At first I'd thought that I was in New York to "help people." But ever since my first days in Harlem, I couldn't ignore the fact that I was the one who needed help—and hope, and healing. I tried to keep all my feelings of shame and self-doubt inside, pretending I had it together, yet I was living in a world where people just acted that stuff out 24/7. They were more honest. I was just as confused and angry, but I was afraid to show it.

I began to develop some unhealthy habits. For starters, I didn't sleep. We had guys with drug problems in the front room, there was a loud Latino record shop downstairs that stayed open all night, and we had no air conditioning. It was enough to turn anyone into an insomniac, and I've never needed or wanted much sleep anyway— that's just how I'm wired. My grandchildren did a skit at my 70th birthday party where they portrayed me saying, "It's six in the morning! Where is everybody? Why isn't everyone up?"

I'm also often tense and on edge, but way less than I used to be. At 215 Madison, it was constant. My mood swings went from "I can do anything!" to "I'm worthless and I might as well quit."

One stifling summer night, I was lying on my bunk with the windows open, trying to catch a breath of fresh air. There wasn't the slightest breeze—but I did overhear Harv Oostdyk and Dean talking outside on the stoop.

"I'm getting worried about Bill. I think he needs some serious help," Harv said.

"I know. He's really unstable, up and down all the time," Dean agreed.

I was upset to hear them saying these things, but I chose not to ask either of them about it. After all, compared to the young men I was living with, I thought I was the picture of health. And to be truthful, their words also reminded me of a period of my life I wanted to forget.

AS I SAID IN THE INTRODUCTION, I'M NOT strong on chronological narrative, but you may have noticed that there's a gap between when I came back to Pittsburgh in 1957 after finding God at the camp in Colorado and my decision to move to Harlem with Vinnie in 1960.

Here's what happened: Back in Pittsburgh, I did my best to fit in. Things with my parents were still distant, but they let me keep living at home. I stayed close to Bob and the other Young Life counselors, and I re-enrolled in high school. The head of Young Life in the Pittsburgh area was a guy named Jerry Kirk, and I'd gotten very close to him at the ranch. Like Bob, Jerry said that he believed in me and trusted me. I hoped it was true, but I wondered: Now that I was home, and Jerry had so much to do, would I ever see him again? Did he really care what happened to me? The answer was yes. Not only did Jerry (and Bob and the others) continue to befriend and support me, but a year later, he asked me to run the Young Life club in Pittsburgh.

I was only 19. Letting a teenager with zero experience or credentials take such a position would simply never happen today, which is a good thing! I couldn't have been less qualified to lead anyone on a spiritual journey; and while I probably didn't do a lot of harm, I'm not sure how much actual help I was.

Your average suburban Young Life club meeting was a pretty tame affair—but not ours. I reached out to the Green Street Animals, and sure enough, they showed up. Many of them were drunk or high, and they turned the place upside down. I could see that it was all a joke to them, but I knew exactly where they were coming from, and I didn't let it bother me. I knew that when the Colorado trip was offered, there'd be some guys saying yes. The opportunity was too good to pass up.

One of the Animals who messed up my meetings on a regular basis was Joe Bellante. He's the kind of guy who needs a book all to himself—and in fact, there is one, written by his friend Sal Greco and called *Left for Dead*. Joe was the real deal, a gangster nearly as hardcore as Sammy Tedesco and his family. Joe and his crew carried guns, pulled off armed robberies, and were generally a menace to society.

Yet Joe was also one of the funniest, most lovable people I've ever met. We hit it off immediately, even though he wasn't too interested in my Young Life story. He and Jughead, another of my pool-hall friends, came to the club meetings and generally raised hell, but they never did any harm. Whenever Joe saw me, he'd yell "Ayy! Magoo!" He had the idea that I was oblivious to my surroundings, and he was always ragging me about it, claiming I was just like the myopic cartoon character.

Sure enough, when the following summer rolled around, Joe, Jughead, and a bunch of the other genuine tough guys came on the bus out to Colorado with me. My Young Life colleagues and I used the same persuasion techniques on them that had been used on us— very little mention of God and *lots* of talk about how many girls were going to be there—oh, and the horses, too.

It was my first experience as a counselor, and Joe didn't make it easy. You can read in *Left for Dead* how Joe typically responded to camp discipline. One of the counselors was Lee Maxwell, a good friend of mine who happened to be six feet three and weigh 250 pounds. Lee gave Joe some assignment, and Joe threw a piece of lumber across the room and told him, "I ain't taking orders from you!"

When Lee disputed this point, Joe picked up a shovel and made him an offer: "How'd you like this shovel on top of your head and the handle up your ass?"

Things were getting very physical when the other counselors came to break it up, and Joe had established his rep for the rest of the time at camp.

BACK HOME IN PITTSBURGH, THERE WAS always lots of drama and lots of activity . . . but running a Young Life club didn't even come close to helping me know who I was. I "knew Christ," but I didn't know Bill Milliken. I didn't have the faintest idea what I wanted to do with my life.

You don't get self-knowledge on demand from God, or at least I didn't. Very reluctantly, I bowed to family pressure and enrolled at the University of Pittsburgh. I was trying to do what everyone expected of me, now that I was being "good." But I wanted to live freely and joyfully, and the college world of the 1950s seemed so buttoned down, so dull. Was this the exciting new journey that Young Life had promised me?

I hated college. My parents hardly knew me. I wanted something very different for myself, but didn't know how to find it. My buddies, both inside and outside of Young Life, were powerless to do anything but watch.

In part, this was because I just couldn't talk about what I was feeling. Keeping it all inside was what young men did at the time; anything else was weakness. In addition, like many spiritual novices, I thought it would be shameful—some kind of betrayal of God—to admit that I wasn't a saint, that Jesus hadn't fixed everything that was wrong with me, and that in fact, I was still pretty messed up.

My new Christian friends told me, "You're on a new path; everything is different." But it wasn't. Many of them didn't want to hear my doubts since it sounded as though I were doubting their take on God. So once again, I was trying to fit into a world where I couldn't really belong, and I still felt like an outsider.

On a whim, I applied for the Coast Guard, thinking I'd just quit school, but I didn't fill out the form correctly, and they rejected me. This reinforced my ongoing pain and frustration about reading and writing. I didn't learn the way others did, and no one could tell me why. Trying to do college work made it all even worse.

I started to have blackouts whenever I tried to read. My vision blurred, and I got these incredible headaches. It was terrifying. Part of me knew that I was having a panic reaction to the academic pressure, and another part of me was sure that I was going crazy.

Finally, I snapped. I called up a friend of mine named Steve and said, "I can't take this. I want to go to Florida. Do you want to come?" It was something we'd fantasized about on and off, but this time I meant it. I threw a bunch of clothes in the trunk of his car, and we took off.

Steve and I made plans to start a business selling ice skates and sweaters. (I guess we thought the Florida winters would be just like Pittsburgh.) But as soon as we got down there and checked into a Miami motel, I just flipped out. My blackouts got worse. I walked and walked, all day, every day. My thoughts moved at hyperspeed, and I couldn't keep track of them. Those three weeks in Florida are a blur to me now. I just remember the feelings of desperation, of being completely at the end of my rope and stuck in a swamp as deep as any I could find in the Sunshine State.

One day, I just walked away. I knew how upset Steve would be that I'd ruined our plans, but I didn't care. I literally started walking from Florida back to Pennsylvania with only the clothes I was wearing. I hitched a few rides and got as far as Augusta, Georgia, although I have no idea how or what happened during that time. I was seriously ill. Through God's grace, I managed to pull myself together enough to make a collect call to Harry McDonald, Jerry Kirk's successor as Young Life director in Pittsburgh, and he wired me money for a plane ticket home.

My brother Ken came to meet me at the airport. I guess Harry had called him. Ken told me later that I had a really scary look in my eyes—no emotion, just staring and staring. I'd grown a beard, and my hair and clothes were a mess.

My Young Life family really came through for me that time. I stayed in Pittsburgh and they arranged for me to get help from a wonderful therapist, Dr. Czickes. He was a Holocaust survivor, and it made him a great empathizer with others' pain. He seemed to understand something about me from our first session. I was in such a bad state, I can't even remember what we talked about; I just remember a feeling of connection.

Dr. C. never diagnosed me. For almost a year, all he did was listen and listen to my pain, anger, and confusion—all the things I'd never told anyone. Then he said, "If this had happened to you 20 years from now, you'd be in a mental hospital. But as it is, I think you've lanced the boil, and all the pus is coming out."

His therapy for me was simple: He told me not to go back to college, but that I needed to be doing something physical immediately. So I went to work in my father's brickyard.

He also told me, "God's got great plans for you." I don't think he meant I was special. He was the kind of person who saw God's love in everyone and believed that we all have a destiny to work out. I know I couldn't have kept going without his caring and understanding.

As you can imagine, I was ashamed and nervous about meeting anyone from Young Life. The rumors were rampant: Milliken went nuts; he's flipped out; he's not a Christian anymore; he's back with the gang. None of that was true. But I was starting to learn a lesson about maturity and growing up: There's no "cheap grace," no substitute for the hard work of faith, discipline, and knowing yourself. Healing is a lifelong process.

"Finding the treasure is only the beginning of the search," the Dutch theologian Henri Nouwen wrote, and my search has never stopped.

As I got back on my feet, the brickyard definitely wasn't where I wanted to be for very long. For one thing, the workers' language was more than even I could stand. Mainly, though, it was tedious, boring work, so I tried selling pots and pans. To this day, I can hear the company slogan: *Ware Aluminum, the Cadillac of Cookware!* I wasn't too bad at this job, actually. I had the bright idea of reading the engagement notices in the paper, then targeting my sales pitch to those couples who were soon going to need some nice new cookware. I also made sure to pick the folks who lived in wealthy parts of town, where they could afford to buy.

I don't know how long I might have gone on like that, but in the spring of 1960, it all changed. Harv Oostdyk got in touch with me and told me about the vision he had of starting Young Life in New York City. Would I like to join him and Vinnie De Pasquale in working with New York City street youth? It was the call I'd been waiting for. I told him, "Sure!" . . . and a couple of months later, there I was in Harlem, hanging out with Vinnie and a basketball.

THREE YEARS ON, EAVESDROPPING AS HARV and Dean discussed my need for emotional help, I was scared but not ready to admit it.

Not this again, I thought. *Why can't I be "stable" like everybody else?*

I didn't consider myself manic, edgy, or angry. I just felt that I was living one day at a time, and every day had to count. I had to do everything I could, every minute, to make a difference in these young people's lives. I believed that the harder I strove, the better I was in God's eyes.

I was still a long way from understanding that I couldn't *earn* anything spiritually. I thought that I could prove myself worthy by working too hard and ignoring my own needs. In fact, the outward and inward journeys are always connected. I can't help my neighbor if I'm a mess inside. We're healed through grace, not through what we "deserve," no matter how hard we work to earn God's love.

But at least for the time being, I was still walking the tightrope, trying to help others, and afraid to look down and find out there was no net to save me.

AT 215 MADISON, IT WAS STANDING ROOM only. Clark Jones moved into an apartment there during his junior year of high school when he decided he needed to leave his parents' house. Trinity Church continued to help with funding, buying bunk beds and kitchen supplies. We now had five apartments filled with between 25 and 30 kids. There was a girls' apartment, too, in a different building on Henry Street. Clark's soon-to-be wife, Edith, was one of the tenants there.

Basically, we invited young people who had difficult situations to come live with us. Butch Rodriguez was a typical example. He was a 16-year-old kid I'd seen around, just hanging out on the streets.

We knew each other well enough to say hello and exchange a few words. I heard from a couple of older guys that Butch's home life was a mess—very chaotic with a lot of parental problems.

Then one night I was walking down Madison Street and saw Butch in an alley. I called to him and asked him what he was doing. Over the next hour, I heard the whole story: He'd been on the streets for five days. His home had just gotten impossible, so he'd split, and now he had nowhere to go. So I invited him to move in with us at 215. That was quite common—kids whom Dean or Dave or I casually knew would suddenly be in trouble and need a place to go.

Butch stayed with us on and off for two years. He'd do well and try to make it on his own, but then he'd run into problems and come back to us again. Anger, bitterness, and a world that was only a couple of city blocks—that was all Butch knew. He always looked up to me, though, and he had tremendous strength of character and really threw himself into the community at 215 and the Young Life club.

Like so many other young men and women, he was searching, desperate for something to give his life to, something to believe in. There were more bad options than good if you lived on the Lower East Side. We offered an alternative that wasn't drugs, gangs, or crime. At one point, we sent Butch off to Pittsburgh to live with the Young Life group run by my colleague Reid Carpenter, and that really seemed to broaden his horizons. Eventually, Butch joined the Army and got off the streets.

THEN THERE'S THE STORY OF MICHAEL ARTIST. One day, Father Dwyer, a priest at St. Christopher's Episcopal Church, contacted me and said, "There's a kid that I want to send over to you. Let me warn you: This one has special problems. He's just gotten out of Bellevue psych ward and no one else wants to take him."

I asked Bo if Michael Artist could stay with him on the first floor. Michael was 14 years old, about six feet three, and a very, very angry kid. I was truly unsure whether this was going to work, and I said to Bo, "You take care of this guy if you can, 'cause I can't handle him."

Bo walked into the apartment the first day, and Michael was in the back room, cursing up a storm. Bo just took a seat and waited until he calmed down. Then Michael reached into a bag and pulled out a hatchet, saying, "I'm gonna kill you!"

Bo replied, "Michael, you don't want to do that. Do you know who I am?"

Upon hearing Bo's name and realizing he had gang connections, the boy put the hatchet down. Then Bo grabbed him, and they started wrestling. We knew his dad used to beat the shit out of him, and Bo told me later that he just had an intuitive feeling that the kid needed some contact, a way to get his anger out.

So every day when Bo came in, Michael wanted to wrestle. That was how they became friends. Michael obeyed all the rules, but his social worker wasn't convinced. She'd come around and say, "That kid's mentally disturbed. You've got to get him out of here; he's not ready to live in a community."

Bo was Michael's advocate. He kept insisting, "No, he just needs some love, some touch." Bo persuaded her to stop giving the boy pills to control him. He'd still have scary episodes once in a while—yelling "I'm gonna kill my father!" and going for that hatchet—and Bo would have to stop him.

He told Michael, "Any time you start to get upset, you call me and come here." Michael would come in sweating and steaming, and they'd talk it out.

After Bo got married, he lost touch with Michael. Then, years later, he took some kids to a martial-arts tournament at Rutgers University. After the matches, a guy walked up behind him and grabbed him around the neck, saying, "Bo, Bo, Bo!" It was Michael. He'd been in the service, part of a special unit that dealt with sensitive documents—and he couldn't read when I knew him. When he got out, he enrolled in Rutgers; and he was married, going to school.

Then he and Bo lost touch again until about six years ago. Bo took some kids for all-night bowling, walked in, and saw that a guy was looking at him. He came over, and they both recognized each other. Michael was now the manager of the bowling alley. He seemed to be doing fine, this guy who they said would never be able to function in society.

RONALD YIP WAS ANOTHER MEMBER OF OUR community who beat all the odds. He was wiry with jet black hair, half Asian and half Hispanic. If we were sitting in the park and saw a little shadow going up a building, we'd say, "Oh hey, guess Ron needs some money." He was all muscle and an expert housebreaker. He could just climb up a building and go through people's windows.

Ronald ended up being taken away to Orangeburg, to a psychiatric hospital that also housed prisoners with mental illnesses. I went out to visit him, and it was awful. It was the first time I'd been somewhere like that and seen the way the inmates were treated. Ronald was pleading with me: "You've gotta get me out of this place."

He definitely didn't belong there. He wasn't insane; he was just dying inside because no one ever gave a damn about him. His father beat him, chained him to the kitchen sink, and put dog food there for him. For a long time, he only ate with his hands. So I tried everything I knew to get him out of Orangeburg, but nothing worked.

One day, a bunch of us were sitting on a bench, and there was a shadow going up a building. Ronald Yip had escaped, but they came and got him again. The next time I went up to see him at Orangeburg, the officials told me, "Well, he disappeared. We don't exactly know what happened to him." I later found out he'd escaped again, then got hit by a car and was hospitalized, but somehow his records were lost, so he was out of the system.

Ronald eventually found his way back to the Lower East Side and asked if he could live with us. He performed an amazing turnaround. This guy couldn't read and was completely unsocialized. But he understood our rules, and he'd decided that he wanted a new way of life. Years later, I was back visiting the neighborhood and met Ronald again. He'd gotten married and was driving a truck, which would be like me going to Harvard and graduating as valedictorian.

ONE OF THE THINGS I HEARD FROM Bo, Clark, and the other Cross Carriers was that they didn't have a high school football team. So we started a Young Life tackle team, the East Side Bears. A couple of guys from the University of Pittsburgh came down in the summer to work with us and show us how to join a league. It was a great time. I also had contacts with Long Island University and the New York Giants, and they gave us shoulder pads, cleats, pants, and almost everything else. The guys had to save up and buy their own helmets, though. We had about 40 or 50 kids practicing all through the summer.

None of us knew how to play. Clark and the others knew the rules, but they'd never experienced it. So I was quarterback the first year—and we lost every game. We never scored a point. Once, I tried a quarterback sneak from our five-yard line. Bo and Clark swear that all 11 members of the opposing team caught me by midfield. The next year, I moved to being the coach, and the year after that we came back and won the whole thing. The Bears were fast learners once they got me over to the sidelines.

The funniest and strangest moment came when we were playing for the championship against this white team from White Plains or someplace. They were older guys, in their late teens—or in Clark's eyes even older. He came running out of the locker room and said, "They're in there taking their dentures out!"

We said, "Oh shit . . ."

"Yeah, one guy has a tattoo that says Class of 1953. They're drinking beer and saying, 'We're going to kill you!'"

We beat them anyway.

What I remember best is how hard it was to get the guys to their games. I'd rent a small moving van and pile 25 players into the back, all suited up. We'd go bumping up the road with everybody hollering and falling over themselves. We'd arrive at the field, open the van door, and it would be like one of those little clown cars in the circus with a million guys emerging: "Here we are, the East Side Bears! Check it out!"

We also started a basketball team called the East Side Trotters. With all this organized sports activity for young people, the Young Life club got really big. We were attracting hundreds of kids every week at the church. And of course, 215 Madison continued to be the focus of our one-on-one work with homeless youth.

ON A TYPICAL DAY, I'D GET UP EARLY and make sure everyone else was up to go to school, work, or their court dates. I went to court a lot and talked with numerous probation officers. And I hung out, strategizing and trying to raise money. (The arrangement with Young Life, remember, was that we had to raise funds to pay our own expenses and salaries, as well as money for organized activities.) Then there might be a club meeting in the evening and maybe a speaking engagement somewhere. I used to get asked to talk at churches a lot—with very mixed results, as I'll explain shortly.

All this intensity took its toll. Despite making my commitment to give my life back to serve young people, there were numerous times I was ready to walk away. I got just as scared as anybody else. *Lucky me,* I'd think, *I get to step into the middle of an Italian gang and a Puerto Rican gang and try to make peace! Isn't that fun?* Believe me, it's not. And guys like Michael Artist and Ronald Yip were, before anything else, *dangerous.* Being in the same tiny room as an angry, strong kid who may explode at any moment is unbelievably stressful.

The first consequence of this lifestyle, for me, was fear. It meant being on guard and always jumping at commotion and the sounds of fighting. I hated any confined space where I couldn't escape, and I never sat with my back to a door. My fear of sudden loud noises got much worse, although it had begun all the way back when I was growing up in an alcoholic home. Also, I'd repressed some of the panic and terror I felt watching guys get hurt by Sammy Tedesco and his mob. By this point, my emotional reactions were feeding on the memories and becoming exaggerated. All this was, in fact, post-traumatic stress disorder, but it would be decades before anyone explained that to me.

Even worse was going to the funeral of some kid who'd left our community and overdosed on heroin. I did that more times than I can count or want to remember. Worst of all was Snake's death. He was one of the first guys I met on the streets, the same one who knocked my lights out when I was trying to teach him how to wrestle. Snake had gone to Frontier Ranch in Colorado and chosen a new way of life. He was back in school, living with us at 215 Madison, and a star on the East Side Bears football team. A muscular, handsome young man, Snake was always smiling, and he was as tough as they came. I knew what a struggle it had been for him to kick heroin, but I was sure he was going to make it.

Then one morning, I was getting into a car outside 215 Madison—to go skydiving of all things, something I'd always wanted to try. A couple of kids came running out of the building and shouted, "Snake's dead on the floor!"

I raced upstairs. There, in the tiny room crowded with bunk beds, lay Snake. He had a belt around his arm. As far as I knew, he'd been off drugs until that fatal day. He probably thought he could handle a bigger shot, forgetting that he would have lost his tolerance from being clean for a while. I couldn't believe what I was seeing—the abrupt, sickening violence of a friend's death.

Someone called the cops, and they came and hauled Snake away. We held his funeral at Mariners' Temple, a small mission-type Baptist church nearby. His brother from North Carolina and a few other relatives were there all dressed up, weeping and shouting. I spoke some words in his memory, but they were hollow. I couldn't say what I really felt: "Snake, I did my best, but I failed you." I know now that's not true, because no one and nothing can keep a drug addict from using if he wants to. But standing there looking down at his body in the casket, I felt so responsible.

Most people who aren't born in the inner city don't have this kind of trauma as part of their lives. For me, it was inescapable. I'd be sitting on a bench in the park with some friends, just talking and relaxing, and suddenly we'd see a guy we knew getting jumped by a gang, getting knifed and beaten, blood dripping all over the place. It was always over before we could do anything about it, but it left us horrified. The constant, sudden violence is almost impossible to describe to someone who hasn't been through it. It was like a war zone, and it took a big toll on my emotional and physical health.

BUT AS I LOOK IN THE REARVIEW MIRROR, I can also see the positive side. Despite my many flaws and hang-ups, despite the sometimes insane environment of the Lower East Side, God did call me to be there, and he did give me the gift of leadership, although it had nothing to do with credentials. I've always been able to relate to people, to listen to them and connect with them. In part, this was a tool to compensate for what I felt I lacked in the way of ordinary education. The feeling of "being dumb" was still very much with me. I had no confidence that I could do anything except hang out, so I figured that I should learn to do it well.

It's so interesting how we develop certain skills in order to cover up our deficiencies—or at least that's how it feels at the time. Then it turns out that those abilities are exactly what God will use to help others. With the benefit of hindsight, my set of "alternative skills" seems very clear. I had the ability to speak to people, both one-on-one and in large groups. I could get folks organized and working together. I knew how to persuade, to present a point of view and make it convincing. The better I got at hanging out, the more it taught me about building relationships.

I was also starting to value some of the intellectual quirks that learning differently had forced me to develop. For instance, linear thinking was never my strength, but I had the ability to perceive connections between ideas that "A to B to C" thinkers might miss. This helped me grasp the big picture and capture a vision that brought together elements from a lot of different perspectives.

Analogies, metaphors, and illustrations also occurred to me vividly and were often a great way to get across an idea by telling a story. This came up a lot when I tried to understand the Bible. I had no training, and the ancient-culture frame of reference was often hard to relate to—shepherds, farmers, fields, and all that. This was even truer on the streets and for the young men and women in the Cross Carriers. If I had trouble understanding something, I would never be able to explain it to them.

When we had Cross Carrier meetings or house meetings at 215 Madison, we couldn't talk about "reaping what you sow." We had to make the agrarian images come alive, so I'd explain it this way: "If you keep putting the hurt on somebody, one of your victims is going to come back when you least expect it and put the hurt on you."

Or I might overhear a guy complaining about "those jive turkeys talking shit" in church. Weren't they supposed to be God's people and help the poor instead of sitting around gossiping about everybody they're better than? So at the next meeting, I'd use his language and say, "If someone's talking it but not walking it, don't listen to it. But be careful not to judge, because we all become jive turkeys at times." I knew this would make more sense than the scriptural language.

I was constantly looking for a strong image that the kids could hang on to. For the loaves and fishes, I used the illustration of going over to Clark's parents' place around suppertime. When Mrs. Jones was cooking, there was always enough for one more at the table; she never let me go hungry. That's what community is about. We take our loaves and fishes and feed each other. I don't know how theologians would feel about the interpretation, but that's what it meant to me: *always enough for one more at the table.* That was the image I could relate to.

The most important of my alternative skills, though, was appreciating that people want to be listened to and empathized with. Young people, especially, need an adult who's willing to walk through "the valley of the shadow of adolescence" with them, and doing so doesn't require a college education.

This was all very well for me, but a college education was *exactly* what so many of our Lower East Side friends needed and deserved. These young men and women had never completed high school, but it was clear that they had the same potential as anyone else. I'm not saying that each and every person at 215 Madison would have done well in college, but that's probably true in your neighborhood, too. Dean and I could see that among these dropouts and "losers," there were many smart, talented, and motivated young people. We were having pretty good success with providing some basic needs: shelter, food, safety, unconditional love, and a chance to live a spiritual life and give back to others. It still wasn't enough.

These kids couldn't live at 215 Madison forever. And in order to make it, they were going to need a hell of a lot more education, whether that meant going on to college or simply earning a high-school diploma.

Like it or not, Dean, Harv, and I were about to go into the education business.

CHAPTER THREE

LABOR PAINS

"What do you know about being poor? What do you know about being black and hungry? Have you ever been out in the cold with your ass freezing off? What do you know about living with rats or needing a fix? You don't know nothing, and I been living here my whole life. It ain't gonna change because of you, ever."

We were standing in the doorway of a little storefront on 114th Street on a chilly night in November 1965. Herbie Miller was shouting so loud that I thought he was going to explode, but at least he wasn't yelling at me. He was aiming his words at Harv Oostdyk, standing next to me, who took it all in—the pain, the anger, and the hopelessness. Then Harv said, "Yeah, brother, Harlem's people *can* change the condition of their lives."

Thanks to incredible individuals like Herbie, who wound up getting his GED from one of our six storefront "Street Academies" in Harlem and the Lower East Side and then helping others do the same, our dream would begin to become a reality. We'd find a way to provide motivated young people with a way back into the system.

In my book *The Last Dropout* (Hay House, 2007), you can find many details about how the Street Academy model worked. The basic idea—which Harv pioneered and championed tirelessly—was to rent storefronts where dropouts could take classes that would prepare them to pass their high-school equivalency exams.

Harv, Dean, and I were well aware that we weren't educators. We knew how important it would be to recruit volunteers who could do the teaching. We needed sponsorships, funding, and outreach. Daunting as this was, we couldn't look away. It was no different from when I was living in Harlem and first realized that young people needed a roof over their heads and a decent meal. I couldn't pretend to care about my neighbors and then ignore such basic needs. It was the same for education: these kids were going nowhere unless they could read and write.

Harv started the first Street Academy in Harlem, and we began one on the Lower East Side in an old warehouse that we fixed up and called the Blue Elephant. We also rented a tiny storefront that could serve as an office, because 215 Madison was just too crowded and noisy for planning and organizing.

We were able to convince a whole cadre of college students from Columbia, Princeton, and New York University to volunteer their time. We held classes on the second floor, but before a young person was allowed to go upstairs, he or she had to spend time with us on the ground floor, learning basic life skills and disciplines. Part of that involved a hard look at emotional and spiritual life, too. These youth needed to be turned on to living before we could turn them on to learning.

We held "family meetings" just like the ones at 215 Madison. The first order of business was to help them talk about the often-poisonous emotions that nearly two decades of rejection and pain had created. And we kept asking, "*Why* do you want to learn?" As Herbie Miller said, "Street kids don't just pass a Street Academy, become curious, and stroll in for an education. The heroes in my world and their world had been the hustlers in mohair suits and alligator shoes who had rolls of money."

Slowly, we tried to instill the idea that "hope is the antidote to dope." The drug dealers whom they thought were so successful were all dead or in jail. There was no hope and no future in that.

All our would-be students were hard-core dropouts, so we didn't have anything like a 100 percent success rate. Many couldn't quite make the connection about why education was so necessary for them. Butch Rodriguez, for instance, heard about the Blue Elephant and our call to get on board the "progress train," but after flirting with the idea, decided against it. He saw it, correctly, as a difficult and often tedious journey, and believed that surviving on the streets was more important. Fortunately, Butch found a path off those streets through military service.

For those who did enroll, we had to keep applying tough love. It was so tempting to be sympathetic and paternalistic, to accept excuses that allowed these young people to stay trapped in their upbringing and in the attitudes society had imprinted on them. We had to look them in the eye and say, "I don't care how bad you had it. A lot of people have it bad. You still have a responsibility to yourselves and to your younger brothers and sisters to succeed."

As for the parents and guardians, many of them were either distrustful of us or unable to be of much help to their children. We soon learned, though, that the best way to get a parent or guardian involved was to start turning their kid around. Nobody has a baby and says, "Oh yes, I want her to grow up to be a drug addict, and her brother will be a gang leader. That would make me so proud!" Parents always want their children to succeed. So we tried to show them that we had faith in their son's or daughter's potential and were willing to put in the time and hard work to make a difference.

I got invited over for a meal one time at the tiny apartment of the mother of a young man we'd enrolled at the Blue Elephant. There was a bathtub in the eating area, plus a sink, a little round table, and a mirror on the wall facing my seat. A couple of uncles were there, along with the boy's mother and various other people, and soon the conversation got pretty angry. This was around the spring of 1968, when things were really heating up on the streets. I sat there hearing "white motherfuckers," "oppressors," and "Black Power."

I was looking in the mirror, thinking, *Did I turn black? No, I'm still white. Do they not notice?* But I wasn't the oppressor they were talking about. Their son had been lost, and now he was back on track, so

I'd earned the right to break bread with them. I wasn't some expert, some counselor. I loved their kid, and now he was making it. My skin color didn't signify.

BOTH CLARK JONES AND BO NIXON became part of our Street Academy movement. "Most of the guys that came up with me," Bo remembers, "you could count on one hand how many had graduated from high school. It was unusual to see anything like that happening. But then the whole atmosphere in the community started to change because kids started to get interested in education. Not just high school, but going on to college. So we started hooking up guys like Clark with colleges they could attend outside New York City. That was a model that other kids looked at: 'If Clark can do that, so can I.'"

In fact, it wasn't that easy for Clark. When he graduated from high school, he went to a trade school in radio and TV, and after that he and his older sisters were trying to get jobs as quickly as possible to get off welfare. Clark started riding a bike as a messenger in midtown Manhattan.

Harv Oostdyk used to visit us a lot, coming down from Harlem at least a couple of times a week. Harv sat Clark down on a park bench one time and said, "You're making money right now, and if you continue, you'll make X amount of dollars. But if you go on and get a college education, you can make so much more and care for your family."

Clark asked, "What do you suggest I do?"

"Start academic work. It's the only way."

At this time, Clark had gotten a different job, working as a clerk in a record factory in New Jersey. This was the old way music was made, before CDs and music files. There were 20 guys at these machines, putting plastic on the spindles, and Clark had to supply them with the material. It got sucked up and heated, and then the plates came down and pressed the plastic into a 33-1/3 rpm long-playing record. It was rough work, and Clark couldn't see himself doing it as a career. So he told Harv, "Okay, I'll try it."

He and Tap Nixon both enrolled in Northeastern Collegiate Bible School in Essex Fells, New Jersey, riding to school together every day.

It was a very conservative institution. The students couldn't play secular music or drive on campus. They were allowed two dates a month if they lived on-site, and the rule was that if a guy spoke to a girl for more than five minutes, that was a date.

After Clark and Tap had enough of that school, I got them into Newark Prep, an alternative high school we'd started that was part of the Street Academy movement. They were two of the first students to take college-prep courses there. Every day, they drove in the Young Life van from the Lower East Side to Newark, and then Harlem kids started going, too. It seemed as though suddenly everyone was into English, Spanish, and all the academic courses. Learning had become the way out, the way up.

THE STREET ACADEMIES WOULD HAVE BEEN impossible without the amazing commitment we received from others who were willing to work with us. By 1965, things were starting to heat up, and change was in the air. Dr. Callender at the Church of the Master in Harlem had become the head of the New York Urban League and was a champion of our work. He and Harv worked out a deal to put us under the organization's umbrella and helped us achieve recognition as Urban League Street Academies.

We also secured funding from a total of 16 major corporations. On the Lower East Side, we were able to do this thanks to our Young Life committee, a group that functioned as a board of directors for our community at 215 Madison. Just like any community organizers, we had to pull together an effective, caring group of disparate individuals to provide leadership for our work. Many of the people on the committee were also members of Trinity Church, which was (and still is) a big and prosperous parish; and a lot of them worked on Wall Street. Julian Robertson, for instance, one of our first and most generous allies, was head of the asset-management division at the Kidder, Peabody & Co. firm of stockbrokers. (Julian, by the way, has continually supported our work for more than 45 years. The founder of Tiger Global Management, he remains a great friend and benefactor to this day.)

The committee already knew what we were doing with the kids. They'd created scholarships for the Young Life camps and helped us get furniture for apartments. So when I asked for help with the Street Academies, they trusted me and opened doors to other big Wall Street firms.

The academies wouldn't have been possible without this bridge to the corporate community. I didn't just call up CEOs and say, "Hi, my name's Bill Milliken. I'm a really cool guy with long hair, living with street kids . . ." And once I met with them face-to-face, I had to use the same relationship skills I'd learned on the streets. I'd start a conversation and see if I could get a sense of what the person was interested in, whether we knew people in common, what his likes and dislikes were. Hmm, he liked football? Maybe I should tell him about the East Side Bears . . .

I found out when I was seeking funds for the Street Academies that it wasn't as hard as it might seem to get support from corporate leaders. For one thing, starting in 1964, unrest among African Americans was starting to bubble over into riots. Wall Street was worried and willing to back a program like ours that promised to address the needs of underserved young New Yorkers.

But even more important, I discovered that corporate CEOs were no different from anyone else. If I related to them one-on-one, spoke honestly, and offered them a chance to give back, they might very well agree to help. When I talked about the things that all children needed and wanted—safety, health, and education—I could see that they were thinking about their own families, too, imagining what it would be like if they had to live the way poor kids in Harlem and the Lower East Side did. I told private-sector leaders, "This is a way to build a bridge to your neighbors." I knew that if they could just see what was happening, they'd understand better.

That's why site visits became so important. We'd take potential supporters to the streets and show them the reality. "Kids go to school in *this* environment?" we were asked time and again. They had no idea what the situation was like from simply seeing it on TV.

Then we'd make a visit to a Street Academy, and they saw the potential for change. Of course, there was a learning curve for us here.

We had to make sure the visits were conducted in a mutually safe and respectful manner. Two things were key: First, we had to observe all the protocols of Academy operation and not just barge in on classes without warning. And second, each visit needed to include time for the students and corporate visitors to interact, ask each other questions, and learn from each other. At first we'd just kind of point the CEOs at the kids and say, "Look, aren't they great?" but it wasn't dignified or respectful. It was as if we were expecting the young people to put on a show and impress the rich folks. We soon learned that the way to make this real was to bring down the artificial barriers and just let the adults and kids express themselves.

But it was the support of our volunteer teachers and social workers that made the most crucial difference. Millions of Americans who'd had comfortable suburban upbringings were no longer willing to take their good fortune for granted. They looked around and saw an unjust, divided society, and they were determined to do something about it.

Dean Overman was in many ways typical of this new spirit of change—although his incredible love and commitment is far from typical. To this day, Dean is one of my closest friends, and my journey over the years would have been impossible without him.

We first met briefly in August 1960 at the Young Life camp in Colorado. Then, in the summer of 1967, after his first year of law school at Berkeley, he and his friends Willoughby "Wib" Walling and George Thompson (who later played basketball for the Milwaukee Bucks) started a Street Academy in Bedford-Stuyvesant.

Getting young people to enroll in the academies was an extension of Young Life principles, what we called "contact work." This meant building relationships with the kids and convincing them to come into the academy and get the education they needed. I was good at that part.

But the classes themselves were all new to us, and without people like Dean, we would have been sunk. Dean, I should explain, is a genius—literally. He's gone on to write some very technical and award-winning books. At the Bed-Stuy academy, he taught a class on psychoanalytic theory "from Freud to Fromm," which was all about sex and aggression. I didn't know a thing about psychoanalysis, but watching how Dean taught, I could understand that yes, sex and aggression were what the young people lived with every day, so they could really relate to the theories. There were plenty of ways to illustrate it for them. People like Dean knew how to create a thirst for knowledge and to show kids that they could do well in school.

We had a dynamic group of people. There were volunteers from colleges, seminaries, various law firms, and investment banks. We'd all get together regularly, maybe to have a spaghetti dinner on Friday night at one of the Columbia frat houses. A lot of private-sector money was starting to come in, since Harv and I were very good at convincing the corporations that this was something unique. We were applying the Young Life principles to the urban streets.

Sometimes our volunteers got more than they bargained for. We had a Princeton undergraduate named Bucky Clarkson teaching at one of the academies, and he got into an argument with a student during class one night. The kid followed him outside afterward, stabbed him, and left him to die in the parking lot. The academy staff raced him to Harlem Hospital, arriving just before he bled to death, but the surgeons saved him by removing his spleen.

That near tragedy had a funny twist 20 years later. I was in Jacksonville, Florida, trying to raise money to expand our work with young people through the Communities In Schools organization (which you'll hear a lot more about in upcoming chapters). We had a kind of town-hall meeting in a church with a big balcony. The lighting wasn't good up there, so I couldn't see faces.

After I made my pitch, a voice shouted down, "Hey, Milliken, it's Bucky! I'm going to give . . . but not as much as last time!"

It was a great set-up line. I explained to the other prospective funders there, "What he means is, the last time he gave us his spleen. He doesn't have another one."

I'd had no idea that Bucky was now an important player in Jacksonville's development, advocating against suburban sprawl. His history as an "organ donor" for the Street Academies made a big impression with his colleagues, and he eventually became chair of our

Communities In Schools affiliate in Jacksonville—both then and now, a valued friend.

So LITTLE BY LITTLE, WE EXPANDED the urban Young Life clubs into the world of education through the Street Academies. For me, the move into education was just part of my calling, my commitment to God. I made no distinction between my Young Life work and the Street Academies or anything else I was doing. How could I have faith without works?

Harv, Vinnie, and I still had our formal affiliation with Young Life, but it became controversial in some quarters. Young Life was about evangelism, but our work at 215 Madison and the Street Academies represented a "social gospel" coupled with spreading the good news. I came to understand that there was a long history of applying Christianity to social problems, and that Christians (side by side with Jews and Socialists) had helped reform child-labor laws, build unions, and raise health standards in tenements. We were squarely in this tradition, orthodox Christians tending to social needs, as has happened for centuries.

Naturally, there was a sense of unease or controversy between our social-gospel approach and some of the original values of Young Life. Our committee on the Lower East Side could see the necessity of what we were doing, but others in the national organization weren't so sure. The division reflected some complicated changes that were going on at the time, both in the wider society and inside me.

So much of the challenge of the civil-rights and other liberation movements was to *walk your talk*. Don't just say that you believe in equal rights; get out there and do something about bigotry and injustice.

I saw the social gospel in this same light: it was a call to action, not simply to faith, so I was starting to experience a kind of spiritual schizophrenia. I think a lot of people can relate to that, though they don't like to admit it. I was speaking at kids' funerals and confronting terrible injustices every day of my life, and then going to churches and listening to Christians say that everything was going to be all right because we were saved. I didn't feel part of that view anymore.

I've always been suspicious of the "ins" and the "outs," who's okay in God's eyes and who isn't. It gives people a false sense of belonging that's based on rules rather than real community. I was seeing that, for me, the Gospel goes in the other direction. It's about grace and inclusion, not sectarianism.

I got in a lot of hot water. Young Life got complaints from churches and colleges where I spoke: "You recommended we invite Bill Milliken, and it turns out he's this angry guy accusing us of not really following Christ."

Some of it was my fault. I didn't "look right," and that was deliberate. I had long hair and wouldn't wear suits. But some of it was generational, too. On campus, the young people always lined up to talk with me after I gave a speech. They had no trouble understanding what I was trying to say. The administrators, though, would smile, pat me on the back, and say, "Thanks, great talk." Then they'd complain behind my back to Young Life. I hated the hypocrisy and wished they'd just confront me if they didn't like what I said.

I spoke once to a church group in Short Hills, New Jersey. They wanted me to talk about the drug addicts I was working with, but I said, "I'm not here to talk about that. I'm talking about how *your* kids are going to end up on drugs. It won't stop in the cities. It will come to your nice suburban neighborhoods." I could see the expressions on their faces: they were stunned, as if I were speaking another language. And in fact, I was so angry and spoke so loudly that people couldn't hear me—the intensity turned them off. I'd taken my raw pain and then gone to a whole other world where they wanted me to talk about "missionary work."

I still believe that it's not possible to be on the cutting edge of justice without feeling rage, but being an angry *person* is different. It took me a long time to see the distinction and to figure out how to use that emotion as a way to connect with people and inspire them, rather than just rant at them and put them down. The flip side of inferiority is egotism and grandiosity, a truth I needed to learn about myself. I was using righteous anger as a way to pretend that I didn't still feel small inside.

There came a point during the peace movement when I was asked to speak at Madison Square Garden as part of a rally with folk singer Pete Seeger and Senator George McGovern. I showed up in my full "street revolutionary" regalia—black clothes, black beret, very confrontational. There were 15,000 nice young Lutherans from the Midwest in town to volunteer for the Luther League, and they'd never seen anything like this rally. Neither had I.

I stood at the podium, and the lights were so bright that I couldn't see the faces of the crowd. I felt as though I were all alone, trying to make a connection between two completely different worlds. I made some kind of wild, furious speech, and the place went nuts. They were cheering, giving me a standing ovation, yet I couldn't tell if they were moved by the Spirit . . . or by something else.

It scared me so badly that I stopped speaking in public for six months. The experience was intoxicating, as if I'd lit a spark but didn't know how to contain the flame. Sometimes words would just come out of me that I had no idea were there, and I didn't feel in control.

At more than one point during this period, I was very close to throwing out my commitment to Christ along with the "bathwater" of institutional Christianity. My weekly attendance at St. Christopher's would wax and wane, depending on how disgusted I was feeling about "Sunday Christians." But I always kept praying (usually in the shower each morning), and I started to accept that there are no perfect systems or people. As Saint Paul says, we work out our own salvation with fear and trembling. It's easier to say who's in and who's out than to accept that we all have our own "shadows" and that's it's only grace that allows us to move on in the Spirit.

The war-zone atmosphere on the Lower East Side only got worse as the '60s heated up. One morning, Bo and I walked down to our storefront office to find the place completely gutted. The cop standing guard told us it had been firebombed during the night. The office was in a kind of demilitarized zone between the Italians and the blacks—or so we'd thought.

I asked around, and the word on the street was that the mob had done it. They thought we were getting too close to some of the

Italian kids who lived nearby and might pick up information about drug traffic. I was frightened and angry, but there was nothing to be done. This very precinct was Serpico's home base, soon to be made famous by Al Pacino playing the title role of the police officer crusading against corruption. At this point in time, however, the cops were still paid off.

For Harv Oostdyk up in Harlem, it was just as bad. He was getting threats from Black Nationalists who wanted him out. One guy in particular—I'll call him Banda—came pounding on the door late one night. I let him in, and he started ranting at me: I had to get Harv out of Harlem, or he'd mess us both up good. "And you'd better not show your ass up there either!" he threatened.

He let loose a ton of anger, all about how motherfuckers like me had brought his people over on slave ships. I just let him shout. He was big and strong, and there was no way he was leaving until he was good and ready. When he ran out of steam, I told him that I'd heard him clearly and couldn't promise anything. After he left, I told myself it was all talk, but I wasn't so sure.

In the end, we never heard from or saw him again. There's an epilogue, though, which is hard to believe but true. I ran into Banda decades later outside a gathering of Washington State leaders; he was running for state senator as a Republican.

"Hey, Milliken!" he yelled. "Can I buy you a cup of tea?"

I said no.

FORTUNATELY, MY LIFE WASN'T ALL confrontations and angry speeches. I was searching for community and healing; and little by little, I was finding what I needed. In the midst of all the chaos, I continued to have wonderful experiences with the youth at our Young Life clubs. We made regular trips to the Colorado ranch, and on one memorable occasion, we managed to put together a trip to a camp in Bermuda. I wanted the kids to see a place that was totally different from New York, and I particularly wanted them to experience a culture that thrived on black leadership.

We had a Young Life board member in Bermuda who arranged a place for us to stay. We raised some money and rented a commuter plane. Goldbrick Delaney, the cook at Frontier Ranch, came with us to make sure that we had three square meals a day.

When we arrived, we were met by a guy named Reginald Ming, who was the head of youth development in Bermuda. He was light-skinned and kind of pear-shaped, and he had a very affected, super-British manner. He came up to me in his baggy Bermuda shorts, knee socks, and white sneakers, pumped my hand, and announced, "I'm Reginald *Mingggg!*" as though I were supposed to be glad about this. I was rendered speechless.

Then he got up in front of our group of hard-core street kids and said, "Welcome to Bermuda! You may call me Uncle Reggie."

I just shut my eyes and thought, *These guys are gonna mess him up.*

But within three days, they were all sitting on a wall, fascinated, listening as he taught them about Bermudan history and culture. They fell in love with him. He cared, it showed, and that was all they needed to see. Yes, he was different, but they accepted him. It was more of a lesson for me than them, since my own principles about not judging people were being demonstrated before my eyes while I was busy looking down on "Uncle Reggie." The kids walked their talk, and I did not.

We got a permit to stay on our very own island for camping. I decided we'd have a scavenger hunt the first night. Bo was with us, and I learned something interesting: he was terrified of spiders. I wasn't sure I could convince him to go out into the forest at night, where large eight-legged beasts were lurking. Even in the compara-tive safety of his tent, Bo was on the alert. All through the night, I'd see a flashlight blinking on and off, illuminating the canvas from the inside as Bo and his tentmates did regular spider checks.

Back in town, we observed that most Bermudans rode minibikes. It seemed only right that our guys should have that experience, too. So even though none of us knew how to operate them safely, we rented a bunch—and proceeded to fill the hospital. Kids were crash-ing right and left because they didn't have a clue as to how to ride the things. The ER looked like a plane had just gotten back from Vietnam. Thank God, none of the injuries were fatal.

For years, the guys who'd been on the trip talked about their experience. It was fun, and it did create aspirations for them. They realized: "Hey, there's something more than housing projects. These people who look like us can run a country."

A lot of our emphasis in Young Life was on providing learning experiences that were different, that opened up the kids' world and showed them new possibilities. Guys like Bo Nixon were natural leaders; all they needed was encouragement. They'd never been out of the Lower East Side, except to Colorado for camp. So we always took them with us when we were doing any kind of presentation about our work, and we always insisted that they speak, too.

Once, Bo came with me to a religious conference of 600 people at a camp in the Poconos. The organizers introduced me, and after making a couple of remarks, I said, "I have a friend I want to introduce you to. Bo Nixon, come on up here."

Bo was sweating and glaring at me, but he got up there. I said, "Tell them your story."

He was looking out at the audience, all those white faces, oh man. I just knew he was thinking, *Why are you putting me on the spot like this?*

"Just tell them your name," I whispered, "a little about the gang, anything."

The point was to put him in a position where he had to speak up for himself. And somehow he was able to do that and talk about what he used to be like and how he'd changed. I know he felt proud when he left that stage.

We tried to include Bo and Clark when we went to talk to businesspeople. If these young men were going to thrive and achieve their goals, they had to be able to sit across from a corporate white guy they'd never met before and communicate. I was always saying, "Never look down. Look him dead in the face. Make eye contact."

I'll admit that sometimes we asked guys to stretch a lot further than they really needed to, with pretty funny results. On one occasion, we arranged for Clark to spend a winter weekend in Connecticut with a well-to-do white family. It was some kind of exchange program.

Clark arrived and met the teenage boy who was about his age. This kid said, "Let's go skiing."

I guess Clark knew what skiing was, vaguely. So they went to a lodge, and Clark rented the skis and poles. They got on the ski lift, and Clark was staring down at the slopes beneath him, really having his doubts about whether this was safe, but his new friend was having a great time, so he just swallowed and shut his eyes.

They got off the ski lift at the highest peak and shuffled over to the slope. The kid said, "Jump off."

He seemed to know what to do, so Clark agreed to follow his lead.

"Okay, I'll see you at the bottom," the kid said, and then *whoosh,* he disappeared.

Clark's mission was: *How do I get down from here?*

He told me all about it when he got home. "Bill, I finally found a guy and said, 'Where's the stairs?' I mean, I'm from the projects, okay? There's gotta be some stairs here! The guy took pity on me and showed me how to make a 'snowplow' with my skis. He told me, 'Remember, fall before you get going too fast, because if you don't, you'll be too scared to fall later.' Oh, great. So that's what I did. I kept falling all afternoon. It wasn't until we were leaving that I noticed the smaller beginner's hill. Why the hell wasn't I told about that? Why did I have to learn to ski on the highest mountain in the world?"

JUST LIKE BO AND CLARK, I HAD MY OWN need to get out of my comfort zone. Back then, the Bowery section of Manhattan was for derelicts and winos. It was only two blocks from our apartment, so these outcasts were my neighbors. I realized that I didn't understand them. What were they doing? Why were they there? So one summer in the mid-'60s, I grew my hair out, got all dirty, and just went to live on the Bowery for a week. It was my vacation! It really was a chance to play a different role, to get away from being "Bill Milliken, the Young Life leader."

I had conversations that gave me new insights. I went into a place where they spray you down for lice and you sleep with the lights on because otherwise people steal your shoes. It wasn't a good place to sleep, to put it mildly. It was hot, and this one guy kept talking and talking, so I asked him to come sit outside with me and tell me his story.

He'd been a successful DJ and later ran his own radio station. Then one night, he was coming back from a trip and saw flames shooting up from his house as he drove down the street. His wife and three kids were killed in that fire, and he just flipped. Everybody has their breaking point. Living on the Bowery was absolutely the best he could do right at that moment.

Some of the other Bowery people were ex-mental patients. They were given one-way bus tickets into the city from the Orangeburg psychiatric hospital when it got overcrowded. No one claimed they were cured or had even improved. There just wasn't any more room, and they weren't violent, so they got kicked out with a ticket to Manhattan.

When I returned from my "vacation," I felt as though I'd learned something important. Here was another group that society had given up on, exactly like the young people I was living with. The Bowery was full of spirits who'd been broken, hurt, and isolated. I didn't meet any evil or violent people there. They were no different from me, Bo, or Clark.

THIS TIME OF MY LIFE HAD A LOT of blessings, but my marriage to Jean Moore was—and remains—the greatest blessing I've ever received.

I first met Jean back in Wilkinsburg in the late '50s. I'd gotten back from camp in Colorado, and the Young Life leaders felt I should be connected with a church community, so I started attending Presbyterian services near my home. The church had a tradition called Youth Sunday where the young people were supposed to be ushers. I was amazed that they trusted me to take up the collection. I had to wear a carnation in my buttonhole and walk solemnly up and down the aisle, passing the collection basket. It felt pretty lame.

I was getting ready to send the basket up a pew, and sitting there in the middle of the row was the most beautiful girl I'd ever seen. She had gorgeous blond hair and a radiant smile. Without thinking, I took the carnation out of my buttonhole and tossed it in the collection basket. When the basket got to the beautiful girl, I caught her eye, gestured at the flower, then at her. She got the message. Blushing, she took the carnation out of the basket and held it in her lap.

After church, I struck up a conversation. Her name was Jean, she was a high school junior, and this was her mother's regular church. She indicated that she was going steady with somebody, but pretty soon she broke up with that guy and agreed to go out with me. I knew from the first moment that Jean was special. But being a typical teenager, I couldn't really make the decision to commit to her. We kept dating, but I kept seeing other girls, too. Yet somewhere inside me, I was sure that the two of us were destined for each other.

According to Jean, she wasn't sure at all, based on the way I was acting. When I left for New York, we saw each other when I came home on holidays. We were supposed to be going steady, but the summer after her senior year of high school, she went to the Young Life camp in Colorado. She met a number of other young women out there who'd been hearing from me, and . . . it got very complicated. Jean was hurt, embarrassed, and angry. She told me that she didn't want to see me or hear from me again.

She went away to college, and over the next couple of years, I persuaded her to get back in touch with me. We wrote letters and saw each other in the summers and on holidays at home in Pittsburgh. By her junior year, we were back together and more in love than ever.

I asked Jean to marry me. She accepted, and I drove to Pittsburgh to ask her stepfather for her hand. But no sooner had I done so than I got scared and backed out. We broke the engagement, and Jean signed a contract to teach in Delaware but worked for Young Life during the summer after her graduation. They sent her to New York for training, so there I was again, ready to complicate her life once more.

We found a place for Jean to live in the home of the Irwin family in the Smith Housing Project. The Irwins had six children, including a 16-year-old named Ingram. He was in our Young Life club but was new at it and still very wild. Somehow he got involved in selling small-time drugs down at the Fulton Fish Market, and an Italian gang took a hatchet to him.

The doctors managed to remove it from his brain, and he was in critical condition for a long time. He survived, but he was never mentally the same again. I still talk to him on the phone every now and then, when we call Mrs. Irwin and Ingram is home from the institution to visit his mother.

It wasn't safe for Jean to come and go from the Irwins' in the dark, so I walked her home from our office and came to get her in the morning. It was a wonderful time of reconnection. I knew that I was ready to make a commitment this time, so I asked Jean again to marry me. She said yes, but that I had to go talk to her stepfather once more for his permission.

After what happened the first time we were engaged, I was petrified. He was an ex-Marine who'd worked his way through college at night to get out of the steel mills, and he was fiercely proud of his stepdaughter. Jean had been college homecoming queen, sorority president, and a star student, and she was heading for what her stepfather expected to be a very bright future.

With Clark Jones in the car for moral support, I drove to Pittsburgh. When we arrived, my future father-in-law was painting his garage. I said a prayer, walked up to him, and asked again for Jean's hand in marriage.

"If she wants to dig her grave, she can lie in it," was his answer.

I took that for a "yes."

I really didn't blame him for being upset. Not only had I broken the engagement before, but you should have seen me—a long-haired street worker who was going to take his daughter to live with 25 kids in some slum apartment. You might say I wasn't his dream son-in-law.

And, on top of that, on the way back to New York, the car broke down.

JEAN AND I WERE MARRIED ON November 6, 1965. She wasn't really planning to move in with me and all the kids at 215 Madison, so we found a place on the 21st floor of a co-op building down the street. Dwight Kellogg, a guy who'd just been released from prison into my care, was living there, sleeping on the one piece of furniture I'd bought, a pull-out sofa bed. Dwight was the guy who first told me about how easy it was to get drugs in prison. He was older, a tough con who looked and talked like the actor Lee Marvin. He'd spent more time in prison than out and admitted that he felt more at home behind bars. But I'd agreed with his parole officer that he could be part of our community. Luckily, we were able to find room for Dwight at 215 Madison so that Jean and I could move in to the co-op apartment.

Jean had to back out of her contract to teach in Delaware. Instead, she got a job at Faith at Work, a wonderful organization of men and women who lived out their spiritual commitment by sharing their lives of faith at home, at work, and in the world around them.

Married life wasn't exactly an oasis from our work responsibilities. We had staff meetings in our new apartment and often hosted buffet dinners with 50 people crammed into the living room, bedroom, bathroom, and hall. As Jean noted, "Entertaining in New York sure is different from the suburbs!" There were so many aspects of our life that were challenging for her. Moving to the Lower East Side, sharing what I was doing, taking kids to camp, and helping them go back to school—she was very supportive of that. But she was away from her family and in a different culture.

Jean's mother was a housewife and valued cleanliness and order, so those were the standards my new bride grew up with. She had a concern with appearances that was important to her and hard to shake. When she and Dwight Kellogg used to ride the subway to work, he'd tell her all these stories in a loud voice, talking about prison, kidding around and trying to embarrass her—and she *was* embarrassed. She didn't want people to know she was talking with an ex-con. When she went to vote, she was the only registered Republican on the Lower East Side. Jean came to this situation from a completely different culture and way of thinking. By that time, I'd already made a lot of changes, but she was new.

When we entered into marriage, we both had traditional expectations: I'd be the provider, and Jean would be the homemaker and take care of the kids. She discovered, however, that the setup didn't work for her. And the belief system that went along with it, the one that Young Life taught about how women should be submissive to their husbands—that didn't work anymore, either. But the whole community supported us as we shaped our married relationship to fit who we were becoming as individuals as we changed and grew.

Money was always an issue, too. Sometimes we didn't get paid because I had to raise funds for my own salary, and they didn't always materialize. We might have to borrow money to get through the month, and we lived pretty close to the edge.

Jean met regularly with a group of young women from the Smith housing projects. She knew all the young people. One fellow would meet her at the subway and walk her home from work. He was sober during the week and drunk all weekend.

Jean told me that she didn't feel afraid for herself, but she hated it when I was out late. Sometimes my street work kept me out half the night, and she was always expecting a phone call from the police or the hospital. We also had a couple of incidents with people like Banda showing up and threatening me. But we had lots of locks on our door the way everybody did, plus the apartment was up high, so people couldn't climb in the windows.

MARRYING JEAN WAS THE TURNING POINT of the healing journey for me. All my life, I'd wanted a close, loving family, and when our son Sean was born in 1968, that dream became real—and even more so two years later, when we adopted our beautiful daughter, Lani, at two-and-a-half months old. But there's nothing like marriage and family for revealing our shortcomings and the places where we need to heal and grow.

For the first time, I was confronted with the fact that emotional intimacy was really difficult for me. I hadn't had much in my family of origin, and despite all my relationships with our Lower East Side friends, there were parts of me—the "shadow" side—that I'd never shown to anyone. It was strange—I could give a speech and refer to my pain and brokenness, but I couldn't talk about it one-on-one. Jean would say to one of her friends, "I just heard Bill speak to a thousand people, and I heard things I didn't know about him. I had no idea he felt that way." The fact was that it was easier for me to be emotionally intimate with big crowds than with those close to me.

I began traveling a lot, too, giving talks and raising funds. I had this passion for what I was doing, but it often felt to Jean as though my work was my mistress. Emotionally, she was really divided, and she was pretty angry, too. She'd grown up in a family where her father left, so a lot of anger about that got dumped on me. It wasn't very pleasant for me to come home a lot of the time because Jean felt so dependent on me, especially after the children came, and she hated that feeling.

But at the core, the problem was me and my own ignorance. The fact is that I was going around preaching liberation and justice, then coming home and expecting Jean to wash my clothes, cook my meals, and take care of the children. One night she laid it on the line for me: "You're out there talking about freeing other oppressed people in our society, but you don't see the fact that you have one right here in this apartment—me!"

I did *not* want to hear this. Jean was embracing the truths of feminism and gender equality, and it took me much longer to see the rightness of her viewpoint. Our marriage should have crashed and burned due to my blindness, but Jean hung in there with me and embarked on a career path that would give her the self-fulfillment she deserved. Today, she's earned a doctorate and serves others as an Episcopal priest and a therapist. A lot of people who know me say that I need both a priest and a therapist, so it worked out great—but this is getting way ahead of the story.

BACK IN PITTSBURGH, MY FRIEND REID Carpenter had taken over as Young Life director. At one point, he decided to load up a van with 16 or 17 Pittsburgh guys and take them to the Lower East Side to spend a weekend at 215 Madison.

The first thing I heard when they all popped out of the van was "Ayy! Magoo!" My old Pittsburgh pal Joe Bellante was still in the gang life, but there he was, ready to see what we were up to on the Lower East Side. It was a joy to welcome him to my (very) humble abode.

This became a regular event. Our apartments already were crowded, even before Reid's crew would show up. There was never enough room. His guys had to sleep in big supermarket crates or else out in the van, parked by the curb. I don't know how much rest they got with all the commotion.

It was a new experience for those guys, all this urban tension. Some of them were big shots on the streets of Pittsburgh, but not in my neighborhood. The Lower East Side was tougher than anything they'd seen before. They'd be quaking in the corner of the room (except for Joe, of course, who quaked at nothing). But I knew that was Reid's purpose in bringing them: real life, in the raw.

Reid had gotten to know my family in Wilkinsburg, and it didn't take a rocket scientist to figure out that the Millikens had some issues. He saw me for who I was—a guy who couldn't make it through college and was struggling, going through some identity issues. I could be myself around him. He understood that we were all doing street work in part to escape ourselves, as well as to try to follow our calling.

Like me, Reid took busloads of his Young Life kids out to camp in Colorado, and we also shared the bond of having some intense experiences in the process. One time he was driving back and stopped for lunch at a restaurant in Lynn, Indiana. Some white guys saw them in there and tailed the bus when they left. Suddenly: *Boom! Crash!* The men started shooting out the bus windows. Reid drove off the road and through a cornfield with the gunmen pursuing. He finally shook them, but meanwhile the kids on the bus were saying, "I'm ready to meet Jesus now! It didn't work at the camp, but I'm ready now!"

Joe Bellante loved those trips to New York and became part of our extended family. He knew most of the kids we worked with, and they used to call him "Pizzaburger" because he came from Pittsburgh. Joe and I would throw mattresses right down on the street and teach kids how to wrestle, just like I used to do with Vinnie up in Harlem.

And in case you've been wondering why that book about Joe's life is called *Left for Dead,* here's what happened: A few years after his visits to New York, I got a phone call from Reid, saying that Joe was in the hospital in critical condition. He'd been shot down by another mob guy who thought Joe had been hired to kill *him.* When I heard the name of my friend's assailant, I felt like crying—it was Sammy Tedesco. Sammy went to prison for a very long time, while Joe had a conversion experience in the hospital that completely turned his life around. A local Pittsburgh magazine put him on the cover under the headline "Hit Man for God."

After Joe made his transformation, he started working with the same kids he used to hang around with, and he continues to do so to this day.

MEMORIES ARE FUNNY. I CAN RECALL specific things we did and a lot of what I was thinking and feeling. But it's only with the benefit of decades of living—and self-understanding—that I can really get a sense of the pressures that were building up in my life on the Lower East Side. I also have the perspective of history. Tension was building *everywhere* as the '60s became more and more confrontational, and people of every race and gender began questioning the injustices of our society.

Just imagine—within the space of five months in 1968, we witnessed the assassinations of Martin Luther King, Jr., and Robert Kennedy and the police riot at the Democratic National Convention in Chicago. Almost 500 defenseless civilians in the village of My Lai in Vietnam were massacred, and more than 1,000 U.S. soldiers lost their lives every month in that war. In France, students and workers combined to launch the largest general strike ever to stop the economy of an industrialized nation. Why not here, too? We knew that something *had* to change.

After Jean gave birth to our son, Sean, that same year, I remember thinking that the struggle of childbirth was just like the labor pain of any liberation movement. That baby wants freedom, *now!* He's coming into the world, ready or not.

"Freedom now" was the story of the late '60s. The words were on everyone's lips, in newspapers and magazines, and on TV and radio. The black and Latino communities demanded their rights, women's groups formed to confront sexism, and white brothers and sisters picked up the beat and began strumming it on their guitars. These "pregnancies" were long overdue, and the labor pains had begun. The Lower East Side was a crucible of all these fiery transformations.

There's a joke that goes, "If you remember the '60s, you weren't there." Sure, a lot of young people allowed drugs to sedate them and blur their memories. But I can assure you that plenty more of us were drug-free and committed to the liberation struggles day by day, and we remember *very* well what it was like.

If you were born after 1970, you may not even realize that many of the attitudes you take for granted—attitudes you confidently expect your country to embody—first saw the light of day as a result of bitter conflicts. I remember having dinner many years ago with Randolph Blackwell, one of the heroes of the civil-rights movement. At one point, his 13-year-old daughter wandered into the room and heard us talking about segregation and freedom marches.

"I just don't understand why any black person would sit in the back of a bus," she said scornfully. "*I* sure wouldn't!"

Mr. Blackwell and I just shook our heads at her innocence.

By the '60s, people of all races, sexes, ages, and walks of life let it be known that they were tired of being treated as second-rate humans. They were ready to expose the system that talked one talk and walked another. They were more than tired of the injustice of the "peace speaking" class, the overprivileged, overeducated ones who were so ready to talk about peace and sharing—as long as it was on *their* terms.

A whole new generation of African Americans no longer allowed themselves to be considered inferior, and they had no illusions that the white man did them a favor by bringing them to these shores on slave ships. Young whites, including me, became angry and embarrassed when we realized that much of what white America was taking credit for had been built on the backs of our black brothers and sisters. We were tired of hearing how bad racism was in South Africa when it was running wild in our own backyards.

Spiritually, I felt as though I were on the brink of some huge change, some new understanding of what Jesus meant to me and to the world. My black friends were asking me point-blank, "What's the difference between your Christianity and yet another system of oppression? You're nothing but a tool in the hands of the oppressor. You come here and work your ass off in the name of helping young people change their terrible ways so that some other white guy who hired you can pat you on the back and tell you what a fine job you're doing for Jesus and America. Sure they're going to pat you on the back! You're helping rid them of their guilt."

I needed desperately to find the difference between Christ and the Christianity I'd been conditioned to accept. In the process, could I also find a new way to connect all the complex and contradictory parts of myself and live in peace and freedom?

Well, I found that becoming free costs a great deal and is painful. I'd been taught that suffering was to be avoided. You enjoyed life by accumulating stuff, smelling right, and looking good. "White, right, and uptight"—that was the name of the game. If you hit a rough patch, a place where life seemed to challenge your preconceptions and values, then you must be doing something wrong. You'd better hurry up and get back to feeling good.

Yet it was in the very process of suffering that I became prepared to fight for my own freedom and the liberation of others. It was going to involve major spiritual surgery, but I would rather have died physically than refuse to submit to the operation. I was willing to be born into a new freedom, but the labor pains had just begun.

CHAPTER FOUR

LIBERATION

The taxi driver was making every excuse he could think of to hang around this crazy house long after he'd helped his passenger get her bags inside. She was a beautiful young model, and as they drove to Brooklyn from the airport, she'd told him all about these great friends of hers who lived in a hippie commune right in the middle of the city and were letting her stay with them for the night since her flight to Europe had been cancelled.

The cab pulled up in front of a four-story, 19th-century brownstone on Congress Street. It looked like any other house on the block, but when the driver and the young woman went up the steps, rang the bell, and were invited into the living room, sure enough, the place was full of young hippie types with big smiles on their faces. So the cabbie was in no hurry to leave: *Free love, man! Maybe they'd start passing a jay! These girls were seriously cute.*

Had taxi driver Phil Green landed in hippie heaven? No, it was only us—me, Jean, our kids, and 12 other residents of our first attempt at intentional communal living. So Phil wound up disappointed about the unavailability of sex and drugs . . . not that it stopped him from moving in anyway.

THAT YEAR—1969—started out great.

The Blue Elephant, our storefront Street Academy on the Lower East Side, was running smoothly. Each day, 40 to 50 guys and girls would come to the Elephant to learn basic skills. If they had a desire to go on with their education, they'd be accepted into one of our prep schools. We were operating three of them now: Harlem Prep, Newark Prep, and Harambé Prep, also in Harlem. The Newark school had 35 graduates of the Blue Elephant enrolled as students.

Two new Street Academies had just been launched, in addition to the six already operating. We'd started some small encounter groups to bring "counter–peer pressure" against the drug traffickers. Dean Borgman began the Urban Training Institute to help young people from other communities develop their own inner-city work.

We were doing something right—but what was it? I had little time back then to theorize, but in the rearview mirror I can see some of the elements that helped us build a critical mass and make the leap from "project" to "movement."

From the start, the most important thing we did—and it never stopped being the most important thing for the next 40-plus years—was to *keep the focus on the children.* In the midst of social chaos and injustice, both then and now, our kids always find themselves in the breach, caught in family feuds between divorcing parents and national battles between political parties. Yet at the same time, they can unite us and inspire connections in the name of love between the most widely divided people and groups.

Here's what I mean: A friend of mine who's a minister was trying to start a conversation with a well-dressed, middle-aged black man sitting next to him on a plane. It turned out that this man was returning from a national Black Muslim event and wasn't really happy to be sitting next to a white clergyman, so the conversation died. A little bit later, the Muslim pulled out his wallet to look for his car's claim check, and my friend saw a photo of a beautiful child.

"Oh, is that your son?" he asked.

His seatmate smiled ruefully. "He's not so little now. He's a teenager."

So they started sharing stories about their teenage sons. Neither kid wanted to follow the family's spiritual tradition.

"Man, it's hard raising kids!"

"You try to teach them values, and look what happens . . ."

So these two men of faith, whose dogmas encouraged them to fear each other, instead discovered a deep experience they had in common. When they talked about their children, those kids were standing in the breach between them, showing them their common humanity in their desire to be good parents.

In thousands of small ways, that's what we tried to do as we replicated the Street Academies. Time and again we said to funders, community leaders, and educators, "We just want these children to grow up decently, with the same chances your own kids have. Whatever you may believe about adults and society, whatever your politics, I know you don't want children to bear the burden."

Another thing we did right was to focus early on *replication.* We were fortunate in having a presence both uptown and downtown, in Harlem and the Lower East Side. So we faced the replication question immediately and had to think about what was working, what our core principles were. "Smallness on a large scale" was our mantra. We knew that we had to keep it intimate but still find ways to keep the movement growing. This approach also allowed a lot of people to be part of what we were doing and interact in a creative way. I had nothing to do with building Harlem Prep, for instance, but many of my colleagues did, and we all got together often to discuss the challenges.

Meeting regularly was about the only centralized aspect of our work, and that *decentralization* was another important element. If ever there was a grass-roots movement, our Street Academies exemplified it. Vinnie and I had gotten the whole urban outreach thing started back in 1960 in Harlem, but by the end of the '60s, it became the thing to do. Young Life and the Urban League served as umbrella organizations for our work, and there were undeniable leaders within the movement, but each new site was responding to local issues with local solutions. Better yet, local leaders emerged to steer a new, hope-filled course to meet their community's needs.

You also need some "live plants" if you're going to do any transplanting. We had a *prototype* that we knew was working, and we could point to the Blue Elephant or Newark Prep and say, "Come for a site visit and see for yourself whether the kids are being turned around."

I also believe that it made a difference that so many of us lived in the same communities where we worked. I could go to a corporate CEO and say, "Where I live, children are really in trouble," and I had the credibility of talking about my neighbors. We were witnesses from the inside out. And we stayed—and kept staying, year after year—although many of us could have left and been accepted in middle-class communities. That kind of *commitment* is what builds movements.

That was also a time when there was less emphasis on data, and more on *trust and personal relationships.* That's a mixed blessing at best, because a lot of unsuccessful ventures could keep getting funded. But for us—a good program that didn't know the first thing about evaluations and probably couldn't have afforded one anyway—it was an advantage. So many times, I heard funders say, "I believe in you. I think you're getting results, so I'll support you." We'd seal the deal with a handshake, and it was such a vote of confidence that we all felt we had to justify their faith in us.

Finally, with the advantage of the rearview mirror, I have to say that *fear and violence*, as epitomized by the civil-rights riots that shook New York, Newark, and so many other cities, helped build our movement in the '60s. The country was going through unbelievable turmoil. Everyone realized that social reform was a necessity. The riots in particular scared the shit out of all of us, including the Wall Street corporations. When we asked them to back the Street Academies, we didn't exactly promise to keep "the people" from burning down their offices . . . and then maybe their fine suburban homes . . . but we might have implied that we could help create a fire wall. Social change arises from many motivations, and enlightened self-interest is one of them.

THERE WAS ANOTHER SIDE TO ALL our progress. My life at home was hurting, not only because I was spending so little time there, but also because of my difficulty in sharing thoughts and feelings, which I mentioned earlier. I was distant, and the time Jean and I spent together was shallow. Every so often there was a blowup, and I'd end up saying that I was sorry and things would be different, only to see it all build up again and another explosion take place a few weeks later. Worse, sometimes I couldn't even figure out what I was feeling—the stress on the streets, my own sense of inadequacy—and I was afraid I'd just pick up and walk off, the way I did that time down in Florida. As I look back, it was only by God's grace that Jean stayed with me.

Sean was the hope that kept us going. He brought so much joy into both our lives. I'd come in late and look at him asleep in his bed, and all the guilt would pile up on me about how little time I was there with him and Jean. Then I stuffed the feeling and wouldn't talk about it, which added shame into the mix. I was too proud to let anyone know how bad things were and how much I was hurting Jean. Around this time, Jean had a miscarriage, adding to our pain and sense of loss. I felt so helpless; I tried to be there for her, but I don't think I succeeded very well.

Yet we thought that we could hear God's voice even then: maybe we were being called to adopt a child. Shortly thereafter, our beautiful daughter, Lani, came into our lives as a ten-week-old baby. We knew almost nothing about her biological family, and it would take more than 20 years before she learned the truth herself. I'll save that story for later, when it unfolded for Lani.

Perhaps the hardest thing to admit to myself was the change going on in my African American colleagues. Guys like Bo Nixon and Clark Jones were now experienced street workers, educated and sharp-minded. They had absorbed the message of black pride, of self-sufficiency and liberation. More and more, they were questioning why our work on the Lower East Side was still directed by white people.

This came to a head when we started a camp for young people who'd kicked drugs and needed help facing their problems before they went back to their regular lives. I guess it was a sort of rehab, although we didn't think of it that way. Black Forest Camp was a beautiful site in the foothills of the Berkshires with facilities for swimming and boating, a kitchen and dining room, a gym, and a library.

A foundation gave us enough money to rent it for the summer, and we worked our tails off to get it ready. My responsibilities on the Lower East Side were keeping me busy, and I didn't attend the first few weeks of camp. Then I got a call telling me that I should come immediately. There were "problems."

I jumped on a friend's motorcycle and headed north. When I arrived, everything seemed fine. I got lots of warm greetings from the 40 or so youth from the Lower East Side who were enjoying the camp and getting themselves straightened out. But I noticed that the counselors, including Bo, were ignoring me. Finally Bo came over and said that the staff wanted to have a meeting.

I said fine. We all sat down, and Bo and the other counselors let me have it: They were tired of being told what to do. I felt an avalanche of anger pouring out of them. Bo pointed out that the camp had been his idea to begin with. "Then all of a sudden, you tell us there's a site in upstate New York that's just right for us, and miraculously the money is coming in from some friend of yours. The decision had been made and the facility rented without the rest of us having anything to say about it. And we still don't have any voice about the direction of the camp. Yet we're the ones who take the flak from the kids when things get tough."

I tried to stay calm. "Come on, Bo. You saw this place the same time I did, and you said you liked it. I don't see what you're talking about."

And for the next two hours, they agreed with me about that one thing—I *didn't* see what they were talking about. But they sure made it clear. They showed me how all the important decisions about the camp were made by me and other white people. The camp manager was a white seminary student. The policy and programs all came from me, Dean, and other white Young Life street workers. Moreover, the campers knew this, and they were losing respect for Bo and his colleagues.

"Even back home, you try to control all the programs," Bo fumed. "You keep calling us your 'family.' But you act like the great white father who gets to make all the decisions, and then your sons and daughters are supposed to fall into line and say, 'Gee, aren't we making such good decisions together?' And when we complain, you talk about how we're seeing progress; we just have to be patient. Well, that's the same line of bullshit that we've been handed by whites all our lives. No more—things are gonna change!"

I went through every standard response in my repertoire. First, I let them see how upset I was, but that cut no ice.

Bo told me clearly, "Forget that meek-and-mild shit, Bill. Your tears won't solve this problem."

Then I retreated into hurt and resentment: They wanted me to leave the Lower East Side, was that it? Fine, they could have it all.

Again I was confronted: "You think the answer is quitting? Then you're even dumber than we thought."

On and on it went. I wanted so badly to lash out or to run away. The guys were getting out all their long-buried grievances. Every now and then, someone would defend me on a point, but for the most part I was getting a big dose of my own medicine: very tough love. Slowly, I began to let it sink in.

Most of what they were saying was true. I had a huge blind spot with a lot of well-fortified defenses around it. I was so used to running things, to being the leader despite my doubts. I talked brotherhood and equality, but if you challenged my expertise, watch out! It was a deeply ingrained part of my self-image, built to protect me from my sense of insecurity and unworthiness. My internal direction said: *Be a take-charge guy! Be out in front! Look good, get ahead! Win, no matter what it takes! Depend on no one! Above all, let nothing and no one stop you in pursuing your all-important goals! Sure, they're about helping others, but they're still your goals.*

Worst of all, I could now see clearly that Bo and the other counselors experienced this as a small example of a much larger issue. They were sick and tired of white people and their good intentions.

I kept saying, "All right, what do you want?"

They kept telling me, and I kept trying not to hear it. I guess the answer was *too* simple: They wanted me to share power with them—not "empower" them. They'd do their own empowering. They needed me to let go of the reins and trust them, to learn to cooperate, to share responsibility and decision making, to depend on someone else to accomplish a goal, and to watch them make mistakes I'd already made.

Man, that stuff takes too long! And it makes the process twice as hard, and the result might not even be as good as I could do on my own. . . . That's the way I thought of it up until the night of my "trial" at Black Forest. But I was rudely awakened. The result of my attitude was that I'd kept the tools and resources to myself, sharing only enough to accomplish the goals I believed we ought to achieve.

Once again, I was learning that intense hurt is often necessary for growth and healing. Bo and the guys had no other way to reach me. They had to burn those selfish values out of me. And in doing so, they exposed another of my vulnerable areas: Even when I understood the truth of their position and agreed to completely change the way Black Forest Camp and some of our other programs were run, I was resentful and defensive because I thought they were rejecting *me*. I couldn't yet understand the difference between criticizing the action and the person.

It's a common problem for many of us: We get taught when we're young that if someone is upset with us or angry because of what we've done, that means he or she doesn't like us and is against us. So when I was confronted with the way my choices were harming others, I thought that I myself wasn't being accepted. But it was my actions that weren't acceptable, not me as a person.

LIKE MOST SPIRITUAL ISSUES, THERE was a flip side to the way I handled criticism that showed yet another area where I needed to grow. One of my hardest struggles has been to learn how to accept the praise and appreciation of others, to know that I have value in their eyes. I placed such a huge emphasis on this with the kids I worked with, but had never learned how to do it myself. Inside, I thought of myself as dumb, incompetent, frightened, and unworthy. Small wonder that I took criticism so personally.

But I did get a lot of praise for what I did on the Lower East Side. If I'd listened better to what Bo and the others were telling me at Black Forest, I would have heard that, too. They were angry with me precisely because I wasn't living up to my own ideals—which they valued and loved in me.

Looking back, I know that I made a difference in a lot of lives. It's no lie that my commitment to young people was—and is— unconditional. I cared almost nothing about money and possessions (although the flip side is that I tended to be suspicious and condescending toward people who *were* concerned about material things). And I learned persistence early. I was a fighter, and I refused to stay down for the count.

But there's a negative aspect, a shadow side, to all of these traits. I believe God was using me through both my virtues and my flaws, and sometimes it's hard to tell them apart. Even though I was a reluctant leader—and I was *never* comfortable embracing whatever leadership gifts I had—I couldn't help thinking, *Why can't everyone do this?* I became impatient with people I perceived as not giving their all or who didn't see what I saw. And I had the additional burden of believing I was dumb, so I'd always think, *That person's so much smarter than me. I guess they just don't <u>want</u> to do it.*

My energy level—all that persistence—was a blessing and a curse. I'd wonder, *Why aren't they more committed? It's only seven at night, and I'm still working. I travel all over the city every day, hustling funds and volunteers. What's wrong with them?* This is a prescription for burnout, looking at people through your hurts and preconceptions. And that was exactly what was starting to happen to me.

The big lesson I was learning as the '60s rolled to an end was this: Healing others couldn't substitute for my own healing. The inward and outward journeys are one and the same, like breathing in and breathing out. I got hurt and broken, and it opened me to the pain of others, so I was motivated to help. But if I skipped my own healing, I wound up working out my issues on people. I tended to create dependent relationships, where I was taking care of the others, yet also denying them the opportunity for their own growth. Nurturing is a natural instinct, and it's fine if that's part of our motivation, but we have to attend to our own healing in the process. I had to learn to let other people be part of the change.

Sometimes things are gray; sometimes they get messy. The process is circular, not sequential, because no one is ever completely and finally healed. I couldn't wait for the hurting to stop before trying to be helpful, yet I couldn't ignore my own pain. If there were some easy formula to guide us through the circle of hurting, healing, and helping, I'm sure we'd all be doing it much better—but there isn't. We work out our salvation with fear and trembling.

AT THIS POINT, A PERSON ENTERED my story who, more than anyone else, helped me understand insights such as the ones I just shared.

Clarence Jordan was a graying, heavyset man who dressed like a farmer. He came from a tiny town in southwest Georgia called Americus. Speaking slowly and haltingly, with a deep Southern accent, he sprinkled his speech with "ain'ts" and double negatives. The first time I saw him, when he was invited to a boys' school in upstate New York to give a talk, I thought he was some redneck the school had hired to take care of the grounds.

Clarence had no interest in impressing anyone, although he could have. He was indeed a farmer with a B.S. degree in agriculture from the University of Georgia. He also had a Ph.D. in New Testament Greek and had rendered most of the New Testament into his own English translation that he called the "Cotton Patch" version.

But the reason I was there that weekend was because Clarence Jordan had spent more than 25 years organizing a Christian community called Koinonia Farm in Sumter County, just outside Americus. Clarence founded Koinonia to try to demonstrate Jesus's ideas on peace, brotherhood, and sharing. The community was harassed during World War II for supporting conscientious objectors, and even more severe problems came their way during the struggle for racial equality. By the late '50s, they were the target of shootings, bombings, beatings, and boycotts. Bigoted neighbors didn't want to see blacks and whites living and working together, but at Koinonia that was the way. Clarence was expelled from his local Baptist church because he insisted on trying to integrate it.

I'd heard about Clarence and Koinonia from my friend Neil Shorthouse, whom I'd known since we were both teenagers in Pittsburgh.

He, too, had joined Young Life and became its program director in Philadelphia. Like me, he was discovering that his version of Christianity couldn't make sense of the poverty and hopelessness that surrounded him in East Philly. Like me, he wanted a more radical, yet more centered way of following his spiritual path.

Our weekend with Clarence changed our lives. This man showed us things about the Gospel that were simple and clear, yet completely fresh. He painted a picture of Jesus as a true revolutionary. Neil and I wrote down as much as we could remember of what Clarence said during those long discussions into the night, when he sat with all of us and talked about his life and ideas:

"At first it was nice having Jesus here," he said. "People were being healed, and he was going to raise some kind of army and kill off all the Romans so that God's people could live in peace, or so they thought. But he got out of hand, breaking sacred laws of the church, hanging out with bad folks, and telling everyone they had to change to be part of God's kingdom. He was costing them too much of themselves to keep around. No system can afford to have people in a position of influence doing and saying things that will undo the system. Either they had to change, or Jesus had to go.

"The setup today isn't any different, except we've tried to muffle Jesus's voice by stashing him in heaven. But he ain't there! He's here! He still means it. He's here to give us strength. But we got to change our ways of living, and that's where it all hits the fan. People would much rather praise him, pray to him, sing songs to him, and even give small portions of money to him. They'd rather do anything but let him make them live and talk his way.

"For most folks, just having him around is okay. But if his ideas are part of daily living, then the message cannot be mistaken. As long as we at Koinonia only talked about brotherhood, peace, and sharing, the surrounding community could put up with us. But the moment we attached action to our ideas, all hell broke loose in Sumter County."

Koinonia was an agrarian commune where everyone shared the land, the work, and the possessions. Clarence took the New Testament seriously and believed in trying to live the way Jesus urged us to. He told us what the Danish theologian Søren Kierkegaard had written: "The Bible is very easy to understand. But we Christians are a bunch of scheming swindlers. We pretend to be unable to understand it because we know very well that the minute we understand, we are obliged to act accordingly."

Neil and I left that weekend on fire to put these ideas into practice somehow. Neil made plans to visit Koinonia, while I eagerly shared Clarence's vision with Jean.

She was as excited as I was, although her reasons were a little different. Jean and I were involved in a small study group that included another couple, John and Diane McEntyre. The McEntyres had moved to New York from California, and John was directing our learning lab for Chinese students. They knew about the struggles we were having in our marriage and with the challenge of raising kids. Jean was able to confide in Diane about how limited she felt with two young children to care for.

In fact, she was practically immobilized. Getting out of our 21st-floor apartment with all the equipment needed for an infant and a toddler, just for an hour in the park, was so exhausting as to be hardly worth the effort. Jean knew that she badly needed an extended family, a community that could be there for her.

So when I told Jean about Clarence and the dream of communal living, both Diane and John encouraged us to consider it. Would we be interested in starting some kind of communal living situation with them? I loved the idea. It sure wouldn't look much like Koinonia Farm, not in New York City, but it might allow us to live out our principles at a deeper level, sharing not only ourselves but our possessions and time. We could wind down to a simpler existence and have more to give away to those in need. I could also see that the structure would easily lend itself to a spirit of cooperation rather than the isolationism of the nuclear family.

My greatest fear was that the shallowness of our marriage would be exposed. What if my wife no longer chose to be committed to me?

Jean had her own fears, too. She saw clearly that her constricted existence as a housewife and mother had her headed in one direction, and it was the path of materialism. Our small apartment was the only place she could express her creativity, which she'd done by constantly replacing all our things with better things. Yet the thought of giving up what little good furniture we had to be used and abused by a "commune" was frightening, since so much of her life for the past five years had been devoted to caring for and protecting our home and our goods. And she, too, feared being really known by others. Would they see beneath the attractive surface to the flawed human being trembling there?

We DECIDED TO RISK IT. WITH the McEntyres, we leased a brownstone at 123 Congress Street in Brooklyn. We spread the word among our friends, and were soon joined by another couple and two singles. Within a few months, a total of 14 people were sharing the house. And yes, one of them was Phil Green, the cabbie who followed his beautiful fare inside, looking for a party. We invited him to stay for dinner, and even though it wasn't what he'd hoped for, he agreed . . . and just *kept* staying. He loved what he found and made a commitment to join us in our spiritual journey.

We were diverse and multicultural before anyone ever used those words: a Chinese law student, a Jewish cab driver, a black guy from Bed-Stuy, a white couple with two kids, and an interracial couple . . . a teacher, a secretary, and a college student . . . all of us committed to sharing what we had. We ate our meals together and chipped in equally for rent, food, and utilities. We also had Happy, a homeless guy with one leg missing, who came to be a frequent visitor.

The first floor had the common areas: living room, dining room, and kitchen. The second floor was for the young guys. Our daughter, Lani, slept in a tiny bedroom off the McEntyres' room on the third floor. A shared bathroom separated their space from the former kitchen where Jean and I stayed. Sean got to have his own cubbyhole, too, at the other end of the floor. The single women shared the top floor with the Reeds, a newly married couple.

Jean was worried at first because she didn't think people would care enough for our kids to make it possible for her to get out of the house and pursue some of her own endeavors. But she and I found a willingness and a commitment to the children that was hard to believe. It was so good for Sean and Lani to have contact with other people. They learned much more from being related to a larger family of surrogate aunts and uncles.

The McEntyres had no children yet. Diane came home from her job at IBM to be with our kids so that Jean could go out and explore some things she might want to do. The McEntyres' dedication to us was very strong, and that was a surprise since we were unrelated and didn't really know each other that well.

Jean also had all these fears about possessiveness. When we gave our furniture to the community, we knew that some things would probably get ruined, and she was really anxious about it. She worried about whether other people would have her standards of cleanliness. As it turned out, some of them didn't, and it made for conflicts. The men's floor was called "The Ghetto" because it was so dirty. I was almost completely detached from caring about these things, so Jean had to carry that concern alone. We judged each other, and it often polarized us.

But the most difficult thing to overcome for both of us was our fear of being exposed in community living. "People think of me as some great Christian woman," Jean confessed to me when we were alone, "and actually I'm intolerant and rigid. What will they think of me when they realize what I'm hiding?"

Although we began from opposite poles, our Christian commitment did give us the value of shared goods, but we both had a long way to come in order to bring our feelings in line with what we believed to be the way of Christ. We really didn't want to be hung up on *things*. We wanted people to be more important. Jean and I had a long journey around this, but I knew we held the same goals.

None of us in the commune were "Jesus freaks," although we looked like hippies with our jeans, T-shirts, beads, and long hair. Our moral standards weren't "free love," "turn on, tune in, drop out," or anything else you might associate with communes in the '60s. The values were brother- and sisterhood and sharing. Jean and I decided that we'd just have to trust that people would care for us in spite of ourselves, because love isn't real unless you can be yourself.

OUR BROOKLYN COMMUNE WAS a practical success right from the start. We all took turns making shopping trips, preparing meals, and sharing the maintenance duties. Everyone reduced their rent and grocery bills significantly, so we had more to give away. Our goal was a community based on need, not greed.

Handling the intense interpersonal relationships didn't come as easily. Just living together doesn't make you into a community. We didn't know each other as well as we'd thought, and all the new closeness was getting on everyone's nerves. We had family meetings once a week to discuss any issues that might have arisen. Conflicts had to be faced quickly and dealt with compassionately and fairly. We couldn't hide from each other when we lived in such close proximity. If we were hurting, others picked it up and often could help us see things more objectively.

Difficult or not, I felt something deep inside myself respond to this way of living. I didn't have a happy home growing up, and I discovered that this was common. I wasn't the only one. Here, finally, I was part of a family that was committed to me, to my loved ones, and to our spiritual growth along with shared principles. I'm not sure that I saw the irony at the time—that this was the very thing I'd tried so hard to give young people at 215 Madison—but I do now. Finally, I was beginning to focus on my own healing.

There were days when I walked on eggshells, afraid to do the wrong thing and set myself up for confrontation. Jean was growing strong thanks to her increasing involvement with the women's movement, and she'd sometimes hit me pretty hard with the ways I took her for granted.

"Can't you find a better way to point out my mistakes instead of slamming me?" I pleaded, but Jean knew how to say what needed to be said. She's since learned about using a "soft start-up" to express a complaint, but back then it was a direct hit in the emotional solar plexus. Frankly, I'm not sure anything less would have gotten through to me.

The McEntyres continued to support us and give up much of their daily freedom so that we could move forward. Along with a couple of the single women, they got up in the middle of the night when Lani cried so that Jean and I could get a full night's sleep.

Slowly, we all learned to see life from each other's perspective. The single people began to see what the commitment of marriage meant. The children benefited from the constant relationship with other adults, some of whom were very different from their parents. There were daily conflicts to face—everything from sloppy cleaning to seriously hurt feelings—but they produced new depths of self-understanding and sensitivity to others. The community enabled our problems to surface so that we could be healed.

Would Jean and I have stayed in the 123 Congress Street commune for years—or decades? Maybe so. It was a wonderful, enriching experience for both of us. But by the end of 1971, we were on the move again, and it was to be the most significant journey of our lives so far. Our communal experiment was about to be replicated in a new city, and my vision of street work was going to change forever.

CHAPTER FIVE

LET MY PEOPLE GO

Our community home in Brooklyn was a huge part of my life as the '70s began, and Clarence Jordan's spiritual insights continued to ignite my imagination. I wanted to live a simpler life, one that kept faith with a radical commitment to the poor. But life on the Lower East Side streets also went on. Even though I was finally spending some time on my own inner journey, that didn't slow down my intense involvement with the Street Academies.

I could see incredible progress as the gangs slowly lost their grip on young people's lives. The change had begun during Christmas of 1969. That was the year the Lower East Side staff decided to have guys and girls from Chinatown, Little Italy, and the black and Puerto Rican areas all sit down and celebrate together at a local gym. We weren't sure if the different groups would show up when word got out that they'd all be expected to sit down at one table, but it was an unbelievably beautiful night.

More than 300 people of all backgrounds came. African Americans, whites, Asians, Latinos, and Italians . . . hustlers, junkies, and street workers . . . dropouts and drop-ins . . . everyone showed up. We didn't have a single problem. After the meal, we turned the lights out, and everyone lit a candle and sang "Silent Night." This gym had never seen anything like it. In fact, a couple of years earlier, two young men had bled to death on that same hardwood floor after a gang brawl.

Our successes with young people were getting us a lot of attention. More and more youth graduated from the academies and went on to careers, military service, or higher education. The major result of this was that we were able to get funding support that would have been undreamed of a few years back.

Corporate leaders increasingly looked to the Street Academies as an excellent investment in the country's future. Corporations such as American Express, Time, Morgan Guaranty Trust, and Union Carbide ended up sponsoring the locations in Harlem, the Lower East Side, and Bedford-Stuyvesant, along with our prep schools. Volunteer support continued to arrive from college students, faith-based groups, and the private sector.

In fact, the Blue Elephant, our original Street Academy, was adopted by Morgan Guaranty and housed in a great new space near Wall Street. That was when we changed its name to "Lower East Side Prep School," which seemed much classier, and it became our fourth prep school.

Our final graduation ceremony at the old Blue Elephant was incredibly moving. Bo and Clark, who were both alumni, came to hand out diplomas. They had started the whole trend among the street kids, saying, "Leave the benches and go back to school! Smart up!" Now they were standing on our makeshift stage, just beaming at the younger brothers and sisters who had followed their lead.

If Bo Nixon and Clark Jones graduated from a Street Academy, nobody was going to make fun of it. Instead, school became *the* place to be if you wanted to be hip. All these little kids were walking around saying, "Smart up!" It was one of the most amazing neighborhood transformations I've ever seen.

At the same time, we started to receive funding from the federal government through an unusual initiative called the Postal Street Academies. Harv Oostdyk was working to establish academies in other cities, including Atlanta and Indianapolis, and he convinced the federal government to put the resources of the U.S. Postal Service behind the project. The idea was to use mail carriers as mentors, teachers, and even administrators for Street Academies.

In so many neighborhoods, the person who delivered the mail also developed relationships on the route. He or she knew the families, the kids, and who'd dropped out and needed a second chance. Moreover, African Americans were heavily represented in the postal service; along with the railroads and military service, it was one of the few decent career paths open to them at that time.

We secured the talents of Burt Chamberlin, who'd attended Princeton Theological Seminary, to run the training program for the Postal Street Academies, with great determination and results. Another old Street Academy colleague, Wib Walling, signed on as director of the initiative.

On the Lower East Side, our successes revived some old tensions as well. When Bo Nixon and the other street workers challenged me to rethink my attitude about leadership, I'd agreed to take a step back and become an advisor, with Clark Jones and Bo appointed as the new directors of our various projects. This was my role throughout the time my family and I lived at the 123 Congress Street commune.

I thought I was doing pretty well as Clark and Bo's assistant, but despite myself I began working too hard, spending too much time away from home, and trying too rigidly to control the direction we were taking. Once more, Bo's friendship and honesty helped save me from myself.

I always told Bo that I wanted to work myself out of a job. It was a great saying, but when it came down to it, I didn't want to leave. I'd helped bring Bo, Clark, and the others to a place where they were actually doing the work—running clubs and contacting kids. I guess I really didn't know how to disengage. Situations came up where I felt that I could still decide things, and Bo said, "No, you can't make those decisions anymore. You said we had the authority, so we want to do it ourselves."

It wasn't that I didn't trust them, but I didn't want to see them fail. Bo told me, "You have to allow us to fail if that's what it's going to take for us to learn."

It was a huge struggle for me to let go of the controls, and Bo basically had to tell me outright, "Stop. No more being the boss." We had arguments about leadership style and how good decisions get made. It got to the point where I thought they really didn't want me around.

Looking in the rearview mirror, I understand it a lot better. It was natural to have trouble letting go. It was like having a child who becomes a teenager, going through all the ups and downs with your guidance; and then he becomes a man and you realize you can't relate to him the same way anymore.

Bo and Clark had their own ideas, and they needed to do things their way. They didn't need me—and that was a good thing, that was exactly what should have happened. If I tried to hang on to my role in New York, I'd just be in the way. The whole program was built too much around me. I remembered what happened with our East Side Bears football team: the Bears were fast learners once they got me out of the quarterback spot. The lesson was plain.

I was 20 when the '60s started, and at this turning point I was 30. For the past two years, I'd been trying to be a parent without even knowing how to be married, with little good example from my own family of what it looked like. I'd thrust Jean into a world that wasn't hers, only to find out that she had her own life. I didn't know what to do next, yet I knew it was time to move on. I was close to burning out, but also afraid of an uncertain future.

SOMETIMES IT LOOKS AS THOUGH life is falling apart, when in fact the pieces are coming together—if we could only see the pattern. By early 1971, an answer to all my questions was slowly taking shape.

Neil Shorthouse's life was also in crisis. His increasingly radical take on Christianity had gotten him fired from Young Life. After a number of visits to Koinonia Farm, he was convinced more than ever that this way of life was what he wanted for himself and his family. In Georgia, he saw 30, 40, and sometimes 50 people living together in harmony, exemplifying Clarence Jordan's values of peace, brotherhood, and sharing.

The farm spread over 1,400 acres, and was a profitable concern, specializing in pecans and peanuts. There was plenty of work to do in the fields. Married couples lived in a separate house, but everyone ate their meals in one space. If you showed up with a car, it became everybody's car. One guy arrived with a net worth of over $1 million. Clarence asked him to give it away to others outside Koinonia; the community simply didn't need, and couldn't handle, that kind of wealth, he felt.

Most of all, Neil was amazed by how clearly Clarence could render biblical principles into contemporary language that was radical and clear. Clarence's Cotton Patch translations of the New Testament were designed to give the old stories new life. They reminded me of how I tried to find urban images to "translate" the Bible to the Cross Carriers on the Lower East Side—except that Clarence was an expert in New Testament Greek and absolutely brilliant at what he was doing. For instance, here's how he translated a passage from Paul's letter to the Ephesians into the language and experience of the people in Sumter County, Georgia:

> So then, always remember that previously you Negroes, who sometimes are even called "niggers" by thoughtless white church members, were at one time outside the Christian fellowship, denied your rights as fellow believers, and treated as though the gospel didn't apply to you, hopeless and God-forsaken in the eyes of the world. Now, however, because of Christ's supreme sacrifice, you who once were so segregated are warmly welcomed into the Christian fellowship.

Whenever the New Testament used the term *crucifixion,* Clarence translated it as *lynching.* I love what he later wrote about this:

> *Our* crosses are so shined, so polished, so respectable that to be impaled on one of them would seem to be a blessed experience. We have thus emptied the term "crucifixion" of its original content of terrific emotion, of violence, of indignity and stigma, of defeat. I have translated it as "lynching," well aware that this is not technically correct. Jesus was officially tried and legally condemned, elements generally lacking in a lynching. But having observed the

operation of Southern "justice," and at times having been its victim, I can testify that more people have been lynched "by judicial action" than by unofficial ropes.

Tragically, we were to lose Clarence himself before we'd scarcely begun to act on his principles. He died suddenly of a heart attack in October 1969, at the age of 57. As he requested, his body was placed in a shipping crate from a local casket manufacturer and buried in an unmarked grave on those 1,400 acres he loved so much. The local funeral director refused to embalm a "nigger-loving Communist." There's now a memorial honoring Clarence in Americus.

His longtime colleague Millard Fuller, the founder of Habitat for Humanity, told me, "Clarence couldn't buy a cup of coffee here when he was alive. He'd have a fit if he knew they were trying to honor him."

Clarence's spirit burned on, inspiring Neil and countless others. My own experiences with the Brooklyn commune were also motivating, albeit on a much smaller scale, and so Neil and I were determined to create our own intentional community. Rightly or wrongly, I felt that I was no longer useful in New York City.

Where could we go? Jean and I, along with Neil and his wife, Jeannie, had many discussions, considering the possibilities. San Francisco looked good to me—I still had fond associations with that city and its role in the social change of the '60s—and Neil made a good case for Paris. But we chose Atlanta. It was Jeannie's first choice, and as for *my* Jean? I have no doubt she was ready to go just about anywhere that would get me out of the maelstrom of my involvements in New York. Also, she welcomed the chance to continue living out Clarence's values and looked forward to sharing a home with Neil and Jeannie, whose adopted children were mixed race, as was our Lani.

There were two strong reasons for our decision: One was Atlanta's proximity to Koinonia. I was an urban kind of guy—no tractors for me—and after hearing about Koinonia, my first question had been, "Where's the nearest big city?"

Just as important, however, were the Postal Street Academies located in Atlanta. Dave Lewis, a former postal worker, and two colleagues had opened three Street Academies in Atlanta, based on our

New York City model. We approached him and found him more than willing to work with us.

So Neil and I went house hunting. Soon enough, we found a large home on a corner lot in Grant Park, just behind the Atlanta zoo and not far from Summerhill, where one of the Postal Street Academies was located. It was an African American neighborhood, although this house was still owned by an elderly white widow, who lived there by herself. The place was huge and had been divided into three apartments with a total of 19 rooms and four baths. We bought the place for $35,000. Today, with inner-city Atlanta a super-desirable place to live again, it's probably worth close to $1 million.

IN SEPTEMBER 1971, WE SAID our farewells to Clark, Edith, Bo, and all the members of the 123 Congress Street commune and moved to Atlanta. There were my family of four and Neil's family of six, and we'd also contacted six single people we knew from around the country whom we thought might be interested in sharing this experiment with us. So one lady moved out, and 16 of us moved in to "the Zoo Behind the Zoo."

Our values were Clarence's: peace, brotherhood (and sisterhood), and sharing. All cars, stereos, TVs, and so forth were community property. Of course, we only needed one or two of those big-ticket items, so we were able to sell the extras and have more money to do things for other people. All our funds went into one bank account in the name of "Z [for Zoo] Community." We paid the bills from that checkbook.

Following the example of the Brooklyn commune and Koinonia, we had weekly meetings—which often seemed to go on forever—to talk over issues. We also had occasional retreats. Living in community is so often about tending to the small things, noticing the minor irritations and resentments that just build and build unless they're aired. Sure enough, our biggest challenges were about things that look simple: cleaning up, doing the dishes, and cooking meals. Cleaning up after dinner for 16 is no joke, and some people have less interest than others in keeping the space up to par. Neil remembers me approaching my floor-washing chores in an unorthodox manner. According to him, I took a big beach towel, soaked it in soap and water, and then stood on it and shuffled along the floorboards until they were clean— or at least cleaner.

Once or twice, I couldn't deal with cooking, either. There was one night when Neil and I were scheduled to provide the communal supper. We were running late after a hard day's hustle and knew we'd never have enough time to make a real dinner. We pulled into a Kentucky Fried Chicken, ordered a million pieces of chicken, then sat in the car carefully peeling off all the skin. Back home, we hid the packaging; put the naked wings, legs, and breasts on plates; and proudly presented our "home cooked" meal. I think we got busted about 10 seconds later. There were house penalties for breaking agreements, and Neil and I surely received ours, but I've managed to blank out whatever horrible duties we were penalized with.

Seriously, the disapproval of our community members was intense when we did stuff like this. Breaking the house covenant was a betrayal of our shared values and hard on our budget. That's the thing about living in community—*everyone* suffers the consequences of individual choices.

NOT LONG AFTER WE MOVED INTO the house, we found our population growing. We got a lot of visitors—people who'd heard of Koinonia or perhaps had just come from a visit there. Some of them stayed overnight, and some of them just stayed. So we rented another house that was adjacent to our property, and Jean and the kids and I moved in there.

The first morning, we woke up to loud cries of "Praise Jesus!" from the place next door. Jean and I looked outside and saw a group of women dressed all in white, standing on the porch. The sun was just coming up. When we went out to say hello, their hard-core Atlanta African American accents were so thick that we could only understand one word in three. But we managed to grasp that the house was a church, and they were out there thanking Jesus for bringing the sun up.

That was one tiny house we lived in. You couldn't move around in the hallway between the two bedrooms without burning your feet on the furnace grate, our only heat source in the winter. And I wasn't too crazy about the packs of wild dogs that hung around all night, prowling and barking.

Soon we had to rent a third property on a parallel street as we tried to accommodate everyone. My old colleague Dave Borgman, Dean's brother, came down from New York to live in that house. We were also joined by Burt Chamberlin, his wife Ruth, and their family of adopted children. It was like a little United Nations, with so many children of alternate shades and backgrounds. We were no longer a commune. We'd become a community—an inclusive, diverse gathering of very independent people who were also committed to each other's welfare.

Grant Park, where we lived, was a neighborhood in decay. The stately brick homes were abandoned one by one as whites fled to the suburbs. We were surrounded by broken windows, abandoned cars, and "For Sale" signs. So one of our first challenges was to stand up against the wave of fear that resulted in the flight from Grant Park. We also had to help organize the neighborhood to protest the city's plans to put a freeway right through the middle. If we could show that people of all races could live safely and with dignity in a changing neighborhood, maybe others would start to believe it.

Living in the South was an enormous change in any case. The tempo of daily life was slower, gentler, and much more conducive to child rearing. There were grass, trees, and sunshine. People were polite.

On the other hand, I was astonished by how open many Southerners were about their bigotry. They didn't gloss it over with liberal apologies or try to rationalize it the way a lot of Northerners did. (Dr. King used to talk about how Northern liberals were willing to come down South and march with him, but when he visited their home states, they wouldn't invite him for dinner.) Blacks were inferior and shouldn't be living with whites, unless they were house servants— end of story. Their honesty was at least something that could be dealt with directly.

At first, this attitude grated on every angry, confrontational nerve in my body. I found myself generalizing about "Southern racism" and assuming that every well-dressed, comfortable-looking white person I saw—especially if I saw him in a church—was a hypocrite and a bigot. Fortunately, I was able to put a stop to this self-righteousness with the help of Z Community.

What about my own hypocrisy? If I was about peace and kinship, where did I get off condemning people I hadn't even met? Once again, I had to confront my shadow side, my "inner bigot" who's all too ready to judge others on the basis of how they look and talk. Shamefacedly, I remembered my first impression of Clarence Jordan: some redneck there to tend the garden.

I needed a community around me precisely because I so often believed that I *didn't* need it. I thought that I was fine on my own, that my opinions and decisions didn't require anyone else's input. By living intentionally with others, I discovered that my bright ideas were no better or worse than anyone else's and that we were all accountable to each other.

Moreover, Z Community helped me come to terms with my perceived role as a leader. Ever since the mid-'60s, I'd been getting invitations to speak, write articles, show up at churches and demonstrations, and serve on panels. My book *Tough Love* had sold very well in the faith community and received a national award, so I was starting to work on another book. Journalists interviewed me and (sometimes) published flattering articles about me.

All these things put a "leader" label on me, which I sometimes mistook for *real* leadership. In fact, all this was an actual detriment to my role and status in our community. I needed to be freed from the leader complex. We had activists and contemplatives, laborers and intellectuals, all living together and learning from each other. We depended on one another. So it turned out that washing dishes was just as important as frantically scrambling around town trying to find one more person who "needed" me.

NEIL AND I HAD A VERY SHORT vacation when we started Z Community. We called it our "retirement" phase. For about a month, we had breakfast at 9:30 instead of dawn, flew kites, hung out with our families, and tried to prepare for our next outward journey. I really didn't know what I'd do, how I could earn money. I hoped there would be a place for me in the Atlanta Street Academy structure, but no one had offered me any guarantees. One of my backup plans was to get a job as an usher at the Atlanta stadium. Why not? I love sports and just wanted to be at peace with myself.

As it turned out, the academies did become my new calling—or perhaps I should say, the newest phase of an old calling. The Atlanta Postal Street Academies were facing a serious challenge, as federal funding was about to cease. Dave Lewis and his colleagues didn't know how they'd continue the effort, so Neil and I began looking for new sources of support.

We knew that we needed to create a nonprofit organization that could be the fiduciary structure for our work with kids. We managed to buy some time for a few months by temporarily housing the academies with an umbrella organization while we built the new infrastructure. Our office for this work was in a tunnel we dug underneath our communal house, eventually creating enough room for a table, two chairs, and a telephone. With all the children constantly around, it was the only place we could think of to get some quiet time.

I spent every day looking for financial support and recruiting board members. My years in New York had given me plenty of skills in this area. It was like old times: once again, I was standing in the middle, connecting the realm of wealth and privilege with the streets. Physically, they were so close together, but neither group had ever spent any time in each other's world or even knew much about it. Someone had to be in between, connecting the dots, and Neil and I did our best.

We met with businesspeople downtown all morning, before stopping off at a gas station so that we could change out of our suits and ties to go hang out at the academies. (Let the record reflect that I bought a suit *long* before Neil did.) Then we'd head home to Z Community to break bread with our communal family. We'd end our days with some more work on our tunnel, like Steve McQueen and Richard Attenborough in *The Great Escape*.

We got a big boost from one of our strongest backers in New York, Robert H. B. Baldwin, at that time chairman of Morgan Stanley.

He vouched for us with Justus Martin, the president of an influential Atlanta stock-brokerage firm, who agreed to meet us and find out what we had in mind.

Neil and I showed up at his office. The security people, not used to greeting young guys with long hair and beards, wouldn't let us in. We had to produce identification and wait while they verified that we really did have an appointment. Then, the whole time we were meeting with Martin, the security guys kept walking around outside the door to the boardroom, eyeballing us, trying to make sure he was safe.

I know we wouldn't even have gotten a hearing without Bob Baldwin's vote of confidence. As it was, Justus Martin was our first corporate backer in our new city, and he opened many more doors for us.

George Johnson was another very successful guy in Atlanta—a property developer—who was upset with what was happening in his city. His friend Frank "Butch" Robinson was the head of Leadership Atlanta, a chamber of commerce group aimed at improving Atlanta's civic health. Butch asked George to go with him to a Braves game one day. George went downtown to meet him, parking in an alley not too far from Butch's office. Four or five young African American teenagers were there, and they decided to have a little fun messing with George. They never touched him, but they did scare the hell out of him.

George finally made it out of the alley, met Butch in his office, and just exploded: "It looks like Atlanta is going to hell in a handbasket, Butch. We've got all these kids out on the streets who ought to be in school. You know, I'm developing hotels in Miami and working in Orlando, where my wife is from. I'm thinking seriously about moving there, even though I've lived in Atlanta since I was nine months old."

Butch said, "Before you leave Atlanta, I want you to meet two guys."

So the next week, George went to lunch at the Commerce Club with Butch and Neil Shorthouse (for some reason I wasn't able to be there). George asked Neil about our work. In particular, he wanted to know why Neil, who was white, lived on the north side of Grant Park, where there weren't any white people. He didn't understand that at all. Furthermore, Butch had already told him that Neil had been the number one golfer on the University of Pittsburgh golf team, a highly ranked amateur, but had left all that to go to North Philly and drive poor kids around in a van or something. So George wanted to know about that, too.

Neil explained that his family was mixed race, which was news to George. You have to understand that George was no racist, just a conservative who'd had a very narrow life experience so far. Neil also said, "In my junior year of college, I decided to really read the New Testament. I figured out pretty quickly that Jesus was not on the golf course—he was out on the street with the beggars and the lepers."

Butch Robinson, as it happened, was an atheist at that time. When he heard this, he groaned, "Oh God, don't bring up that Jesus stuff!"

But Neil went on to say that the lepers of today are children who can't read and write. He told George some very moving stories about kids he'd worked with in Philly and made a strong case that the same kind of approach could turn around the deterioration of Atlanta's schools and keep dropouts off the streets.

I met George a week or so later. In between, though, he got hold of both my books, *Tough Love* and *So Long, Sweet Jesus*, and read them. In *So Long, Sweet Jesus* there were some things that disturbed him terribly, mainly the passages where I challenged the power of corporations and some of the aspects of American capitalism, using colorful language you don't often see in a book distributed by a Christian publisher. And of course, George was a conservative Southern Baptist, so my take on Jesus was upsetting to him. All in all, he'd decided I was probably a Communist. He liked what Neil had been saying, but he was determined to straighten me out before he could even consider supporting our work.

Neil had told him we didn't have cars, so George called me and said, "I'll come pick you up, and we can have a talk."

He came by the next morning during a huge rainstorm. Neither of us had umbrellas, so we sat there, soaked, in George's car for at least two hours. He started off questioning me about the book, but I knew better than to debate theology with him. Instead, I told him the story of my own life and experiences, how I was trying to give back what had been given to me, and how the young people in Atlanta needed adults to rally around them.

George told me later, "I was probably too much into my own ego to believe someone else was influencing me . . . but you were." He said that his thinking started to change from that day, and a few months later when he was at dinner with his family, his brother said, "George is beginning to sound like a Communist."

WE ENDED UP INCORPORATING the academies under a new name, Exodus. Neil wanted a name that symbolized the idea of leading people out of bondage, since that was certainly what we wanted to do for the dropouts of Atlanta. We also wanted to appeal to Christians and Jews alike. "Exodus" was perfect, and the academies and their offshoots operated in Atlanta under that name for the next 30 years.

I thought that I was good at building bridges, making friends, and creating partnerships, but Neil was a genius. He saw opportunities in places I never dreamed of. He got us foundation grants, city-government funds, and personal loans; and somehow we were able to pay our tiny staff each week. We built a board of directors that included George Johnson, who was looking to get more involved, although he told us frankly that he still wasn't absolutely sure if we were for real or just talk. But the more he saw, the more he was willing to stick with us.

I soon found that working with dropouts in Atlanta was not greatly different from what I'd experienced in New York. There was less tension between black and white—Dave Lewis, for instance, who was African American, never made us feel like unwelcome carpetbaggers, and he had as much black pride as anyone I ever met. It was just a slightly different attitude, a sense that we all had to pull together for the kids' sake. To my relief, there was less of a serious drug problem as well. A lot of our academy students were struggling with pot and alcohol, but heroin wasn't omnipresent.

Overall, though, Neil and I found the same desperate conditions among Atlanta's poor families. If you were a high-school dropout, there was little work for you and no future. But hundreds of young people were ready to jump at the chance for a new start. The academies gave them a way back in, a way to pass their high-school equivalency test and get back on track. Our teachers were a combination of Z Community volunteers, college students, and mail carriers recruited by Dave Lewis.

Sometimes it was possible to use the "leader" label to good effect, especially if it led to connections that could help kids. As Exodus began to receive some attention, I was startled to find myself invited to join Leadership Atlanta. I have no idea how I was nominated. It seemed like this kind of organization always picked a priest, a rabbi, and a wacko. That year I was the wacko. (Neil got to be the nominated wacko the following year.)

After the introductory meeting ended, the nominated priest— yes, there really was one—said to me, "Hey, let's get out of here and get a drink." He was Tom Bowers, rector of St. Luke's Episcopal, a big downtown church. I discovered that Tom was in the process of shaking up this long-established, staid parish. He told his congregation, "This isn't a social club—we're about the poor and oppressed," and proceeded to walk his talk.

Jean had been saying that we really needed to pick a church, for the sake of Sean and Lani. After meeting Tom, I figured, _If they let this guy in, they'll let anybody join._ So we did, and Jean soon began to feel a tug to study theology, never thinking at the time that she might one day become a priest herself. But within a short time, she was attending seminary.

In December of 1971, I was meeting with a school principal one morning about a young man who'd dropped out and was now at one of the Street Academies. A note was passed in: there was a phone call for me. I excused myself and left the principal's office to take the call on his secretary's phone. The voice on the other end said something about being with a hospital, and then I heard the words, the ones every parent prays never to hear: "Your son was run over by a car. He's in critical condition. We don't think he's going to make it." It was the day after Sean's third birthday.

Neil got me to the hospital, where a frantic Jean was waiting for me. Our Sean was being worked on by a team of emergency-room doctors. Not five minutes after I ran in, I was holding him down while they cut two holes into his chest to insert tubes—a lung had collapsed.

I can't remember when I pieced together what had happened, but this is the story: A woman named Sissy from the commune was driving Jean and Sean on a nearby highway, with Jean in the passenger seat and Sean in the back. Safety standards were a lot less stringent in 1971—child safety locks hadn't been invented, car seats were only for infants, and seat-belt use, not being mandatory, was spotty at best.

So Sean was playing with a three-wheeler toy on the backseat, and he accidentally pushed it against the door handle. The door flew open, and Sean tumbled onto the highway, where the car behind them ran over him. Another car driving by managed to stop within inches of crushing his head.

When the paramedics brought him in, Sean's vital signs were dropping, and the doctors feared massive internal and brain injuries in addition to the obvious broken bones. There were tire marks across his stomach and chest. They couldn't even give Sean an anesthetic when they stuck those tubes in him because they were afraid his spleen was ruptured and his body wouldn't be able to handle the drug.

Sean stayed alive that first hour, then the next and the next. As the word spread about the accident, a prayer chain began at St. Luke's that reached out to friends and strangers across the country. Flowers arrived from all over, including a bouquet from the backup quarterback for the Atlanta Falcons. We couldn't figure out why until we read the note and discovered that he was the guy driving the car that nearly ran over Sean's head.

Sean wasn't doing well. At one point, his lung collapsed again, but the doctors kept him going. Jean and I didn't leave his side as the hours stretched into days, with no clear sign of whether he'd make it or not. Tom Bowers came and anointed him with oil. I was a basket case, refusing to go to sleep because the doctors had leveled with us.

"He could go any time," they said.

During the third or fourth night, all the monitors hooked up to Sean suddenly started beeping. I could see blood starting to run through the tubes in his side. The desperate doctor on duty muttered that Sean's spleen had probably burst. I put my head under the oxygen tent and grabbed my son.

"Sean," I whispered through my tears, "do you believe Jesus can make you better?"

I wasn't sure he was hearing me—his eyes were glazed—but then he sat up and said, "Daddy, he already is."

All at once, the crisis passed. Within 24 hours, Sean was out of intensive care, his temperature down from 105 to 99. All the bleeding had stopped, and he was able to take his first sip of water.

His doctor heard my story and replied, "I'm not really into God or anything, but I've never seen a recovery like this one."

Ten days later, Sean came home for Christmas with Jean's family in Pittsburgh.

This is my own personal miracle story, which I credit to the dozens of our friends and family who were lighting candles and praying constantly for our son's recovery. When I saw him coming down the stairs on Christmas morning, I let all that fear and gratitude flood out in tears. The holiday presents meant nothing—this was the only gift I needed. And for years, I woke up on the anniversary of the day Sean was hit, drenching the sheets with sweat, trembling, reliving it.

Sean doesn't remember any of it, although he can look in the mirror and see the scars from where they put tubes into him without anesthetic. As for me, writing about it still makes me sick to my stomach.

JEAN AND I MANAGED TO find our balance again after Sean's accident, although it took months to work through the pain and fear. Gradually, I was able to get my head back into street work, and the future of the Street Academies.

Neil, Dave Lewis, and I decided to approach Dr. Alonzo Crim, the superintendent of schools, about repositioning public-school teachers into our academies. Dr. Crim was new on the job, the first African American to head a major Southern school system, and open to new ideas. He knew and respected Dave Lewis and was willing to give us a chance. So then we had teachers who were being paid by somebody else—the city—but operating under our leadership.

The next step may seem inevitable now, but it wasn't then. Why not bring our work into the schools themselves? Why not reach the young people *before* they dropped out, and offer them whatever support they needed to stay in school and graduate? This was the defining moment for us, the beginning of what was to become the national Communities In Schools movement, and the culmination of my life's journey so far.

In the rearview mirror, I can see how all the lessons learned in the '60s—about community, safety, and the importance of personal relationships—came together in this decision. More than any other single point, this was the beginning of a *national* movement that could replicate and strengthen all our preceding work. Only by going inside the public schools could we link ourselves with a system that had a chance of reaching the millions of young people in jeopardy of dropping out.

Our principles had never changed—that, too, seems very clear when I look back. Think about the Young Life clubs, which were flourishing in the '50s when I first became involved in *that* national movement. Young Life founder Jim Rayburn didn't know the power of what he'd discovered, in my opinion. If you analyze his theology, it wasn't much different from your average Baptist church down the street. But his *sociology* was innovative, because it emphasized "contact work," reaching out to young people where they were, rather than expecting the kids to come to church.

When we applied this idea to the urban Young Life movement, we turned contact work into street work—same sociological principle, different application. It was still about connecting with kids on their own level and learning to understand their particular needs and love them unconditionally.

Or consider how the urban Young Life clubs emphasized safety for their young members. If you're a recovering junkie, this is about a safe physical place and people to watch your back and support you, one day at a time. If you're on probation and you get caught in a bar, you go back to prison. So you need boundaries, and that's why we formed groups like the Cross Carriers. It wasn't to create a pious, fundamentalist club to tell you what's right and wrong. That was never our approach.

We offered simple rules and structures designed to be useful: stay out of bars, don't hang out on dangerous corners, have discipline and schedules in your life on a daily basis. We didn't offer these rules *because* they were rules; it was never legalistic and right versus wrong. It was all about helping the young people to grow and know they were loved. They needed to feel safe—literally safe—to know they weren't in imminent danger of being killed or getting back on junk or returning to prison.

Flash forward to Atlanta in the early '70s. Safety was still a big issue in the city's public schools, only by now we'd realized this meant so much more than just physical safety. Part of me knew this all along.

School wasn't safe for me as someone who learned differently. If you raise your hand and get put down for being dumb, that's as wounding and violent as being punched in the face. And when you're wounded in this way, you internalize it, especially if you grow up in a culture that says, "Keep it inside, don't admit you're hurt." It turns to fear and paralysis of the soul. You become reactive, saying, "I'm not going to *let* myself hurt. If you put me down, I'm getting out of here, or else I'm going to hurt you right back."

So we still needed to create a safe place for kids, all these years later. The principle hadn't changed; only the application was different and much broader. Psychological and emotional safety were now just as significant to us as physical security—not that it was overlooked. Whether from gangs or bullying, a school can still be a dangerous place unless adults intervene.

Next, consider our idea that services needed to be coordinated in one place: the public school. Ever since Harv, Dean, and I first began trying to meet the needs of urban youth, *coordination of services* was desperately important to us—we just didn't use the term. The experience was much more hands-on, and much more frustrating.

There we were at 215 Madison, and kids living with us had rotting teeth, tough probation officers who didn't know the whole picture, and drug problems. I drove around all day, taking them in the van to 50 different places, fighting these bureaucracies to try to get them help. I sat in court, wondering, *Should I take this kid to Teen Challenge because he's Hispanic? No, we've got to take him back to the walk-in clinic first for a tetanus shot (cheap tennis shoes and broken glass are a bad combination), and they close at four o'clock . . .*

I kept thinking, *Man, there's got to be some other way.*

So we didn't call it "coordination of services" or "integrating resource delivery" in the Street Academies. We were just asking, "Why don't we get the services to come to *us*?" But it didn't happen all of a sudden, and there was no amazing conceptual lightbulb that went on, telling us: "Wow, okay, now we're doing integration of services around schools!"

The question was: "How the hell do you deal with abscessed teeth and focus on learning? No wonder she can't concentrate on schoolwork."

Another insight that came together in this process was thinking about how families handle the service-coordination issue. I went to people's homes to try to get help for 215 Madison and, as I sat at the kitchen table talking, I'd realize that Mrs. Smith was accomplishing for her own children all the things that I was doing for our residents. Did they need a dentist and shoes? She located whatever help they required, and that was her job. But our street kids didn't have that advocate, or else they had parents who were working two jobs and didn't know how to "work the system" anyway.

This became a big realization: All I wanted for our kids was the same resources that others wanted for *their* children, delivered in the same timely way. But when we spelled that out and tried to institutionalize it and replicate it in a public system, it became "coordination of services."

Another principle that we had to weave into the fabric that became Communities In Schools was focus on the individual youth, which to us meant caring about him or her spiritually. In Harlem in 1960, Vinnie and I believed that every child had a right to a roof over his head and a decent meal. In Atlanta in 1973, Neil and I believed that every child could learn and deserved the same chance at the starting line in school. Our vision of the infinite, precious value of one young life was always the same—we just kept finding larger and larger ways to apply it. And sometimes it was difficult to keep going, because the more hurt and need we discovered, the more upsetting and frustrating it could be.

I'M A STRONG BELIEVER IN THE SEPARATION of church and state, and I don't want any child of mine being told how or when to worship. But to go from that idea to thinking that we can separate the spiritual from the rest of education—that's impossible. Growing up healthy means thriving mentally, physically, emotionally, and spiritually. I never saw any boundaries there, and I don't know how someone could draw them in practice.

In Atlanta, Neil and I never thought, *Oh, we're in the public schools now, we have to be secular.* Because it's not as though we were evangelizing children in the first place or trying to get them to join a place of worship. Our spiritual principles were being lived out in a new context—a public high school—and we didn't experience that as a conflict at all. Neither did anyone else, including teachers, principals, and school superintendents. It's never been an issue.

When principles are truly flexible and based on spiritual understanding, they free us instead of trapping us in legalistic structures. The two strongest principles for living that I know of are: "Love God with all your heart and soul and strength and mind," and "Love your neighbor as yourself." Everything else grows out of these ideas, and they also provide the *reason* for the more visible stuff such as structures or boundaries.

If I obey the law that says "Do not steal," it's not because I wouldn't like to take things sometimes. And I'm not motivated by the thought, *Well, God said so and that's the end of the story.* I act this way because I can't love you and then steal from you. There's a *reason* why robbery goes against the idea of love. We want for our neighbor what we want for ourselves.

Everything comes from grace. Obeying laws won't get us into heaven. We're all in the same boat, equally and thoroughly messed up, full of flaws, sins, and self-doubt. I don't know any way to "justify" or "save" people, other than finding a way to love them as I do myself.

Reflecting on this, I remember a plane trip I made a couple of years ago. The guy next to me was reading a Bible. He kept saying hello and trying to engage me in conversation, but I just smiled and kept my earphones on. At this point in my life, I really don't like being witnessed to. We were circling Los Angeles for 30 or 40 minutes, and finally I had to leave the privacy of my music and go to the bathroom.

When I got back to my seat, the guy said, very humbly, "Hey, let me just talk to you for a minute."

So I let him speak his witness. It was the standard approach: legalistic, right versus wrong, saved versus damned, heaven versus hell, my way or the highway. I have to hand it to him—he was very systematic. He had all the points down in the right order: one two three. We finally landed, by which time I was more than ready to get off.

As we were preparing to file out, the man said, "So—do you believe Jesus is the answer?"

I let a little silence build up, and then I said, "Not really. I think he's the *question*. What do *you* think?"

He didn't know what to do, because I'd thrown him off his linear system. That guy could not wait to get away from me. He'd been brainwashed. He was trying to manipulate God to produce these simple answers that gave him the assurance he was going to heaven. If Jesus is the answer, then you've put God in a little box. But if he's the question, we have to keep exploring, doubting, and growing in faith.

I once attended a jazz worship service conducted by a gifted preacher, Reverend Dan Matthews. All the hymns and lectionary—even the sermon—were expressed in the language of this music, both vocally and instrumentally. It was incredibly moving, and I had a realization: My faith is like jazz. I take two "themes"—"love the Lord" and "love your neighbor as yourself"—and improvise all the rest. You can play almost anything with those themes.

This isn't accepted in a lot of faith circles, but I realized that's what I've always done—I play jazz. The notes aren't on the page. There are only those two boundaries, and anything else we play that elaborates on the themes is fine. Jazz asks us to be real, to not conform, to be ourselves. In that realness, the music will come. And of course, jazz always has a little bit of the blues. It's music that comes out of pain.

The other great thing about it is that every instrument is valued for itself. Maybe I can't play drums or I'm not as good on the trumpet as someone else, but that's okay. My instrument is my gift that I alone can bring, and we all play off each other.

So often with institutional religion, everyone's supposed to be the same. We're only allowed a couple of instruments. Those saxes and marimbas aren't "scriptural" because they're outside the institution's range of experience. Inevitably, only a few people get really good at the particular official instruments, and the rest of us feel unvalued. As far as I'm concerned, some people are good at reading music and some prefer to improvise, and there's no right or wrong about it. Let's all play off each other and increase that joyful noise.

SOME THINGS STAND OUT VERY clearly in the rearview mirror. Looking back, it's so easy for me to see how these ideas were coming together in Atlanta in the early '70s.

At the time, though, all Neil, Dave, and I had was our dream: to affect the whole community by using the schools as anchors. We were elated by our successes in Atlanta and thought we could take on everything. The three of us would sit around musing, "Okay, what should we do after we turn the schools around?" We felt that we could create a "small wheel" in schools that would eventually turn a much bigger wheel and transform communities. We called this project the "Institutional Development Corporation," which captured the idea but was maybe the dullest and most confusing name for an organization ever invented.

Not all of our colleagues shared this dream. A number of the academy staff were unhappy about the idea of putting our movement to work inside the school system. "The bureaucracy will take over and the whole thing will die," they assured us.

It seemed that my move to Atlanta hadn't freed me from confrontations. I found myself constantly on the defensive about this new vision. Everybody wanted change—unless *they* had to make a shift. Then, all at once, they turned conservative, warning about the dangers of new ideas. I guess it's just human nature.

Anyway, we first had to get ourselves into the public schools. We were already halfway in, thanks to the assignment of public-school teachers into our academies. We approached Dr. Crim, and he gave us the go-ahead to bring Exodus into two high schools. He arranged for us to work with 82 young people, basically the 82 most troubled students in Atlanta.

The first school shall remain nameless, and so shall its principal, who couldn't stand us. He was a former Marine drill sergeant. He didn't believe in our approach and didn't want us in his school. But the superintendent had told him he had to cooperate with us, so he put on a genial false front and then knifed us in the back whenever he could.

Sadly, this wasn't just a philosophical difference between us. He was a do-nothing principal who let his students sign in when they arrived in the morning and then leave. That way he could present excellent attendance numbers and pretend he was educating kids. Being the radicals we were, Neil, Dave, and I had the nerve to notice things like that.

Nameless High School kicked us out after six months. It was a foregone conclusion, given the administrator's attitude, and we saw it coming. I asked our friend and board member George Johnson to try to intervene whenever the principal got mad at us. George would go down to the school with a couple of sandwiches and talk to the guy and calm him down, but we knew that sooner or later, we'd get the boot.

The other place that Dr. Crim had invited us into, Smith High School, had proved a much more welcoming place, so we made a plan to march all our kids across the park from Nameless to Smith as soon as they booted us out. Not for nothing were we called Exodus, and we turned the whole thing into a victory march. Within a year, Smith became our best demonstration site. I hope anyone who wants to try something new and is worried about failing will take a lesson from this: One failure means nothing. Perseverance is everything.

We were also operating four Street Academies, as well as an academy at St. Luke's. So Neil, Dave, and I felt we had a prototype that could be replicated in other communities. People in positions of influence continued to speak up on our behalf. In addition to Justus Martin and George Johnson, we had a great ally in Anne Cox Chambers, chair of Atlanta Newspapers and later publisher of *The Atlanta Journal-Constitution* and director of Cox Enterprises. Ann Cramer, with the assistance of her husband Jeff, became part of our team as an on-loan executive from IBM. And Neil's assistant, Patty Pflum, brought her incredible talents to the cause.

Up until then, we'd been regarded outside Atlanta as energetic idealists at best and upstart hippie radicals at worst. We kept getting this infuriating catch-22 reaction from potential funders. We'd say, "Please fund us to expand our prototype to new communities so that we can prove our theory that the principles can apply in many different circumstances and settings."

And they'd say, "We've never heard of this approach before. We'll give you money once you've replicated it and shown that it can be done."

And we'd say, "But we don't *have* any money to replicate—that's the whole problem!"

And they'd say, "Well, come back when you're more established."

It was like a bank manager who says, "I'll give you a loan as soon as you can demonstrate you don't really need it."

One foundation head told me, "Bill, we're worried that this thing is built on charisma and unusually dedicated people."

I nearly snapped his head off. "Are you telling me that all the 'unusually dedicated people' in the country work in four schools in Atlanta? The whole point of replication is that it's not about us. Any community leader can use our principles."

I BEGAN TO SINK INTO depression. I could hardly force myself out of bed each morning, and I wasn't sleeping more than a few hours a night. Jean, Sean, Lani, and I had moved into that tiny house, and after they all went to sleep, I sat out front wondering, *What's next? Where am I going?*

For the first time in my life, I began drinking to self-medicate. It was the same pattern I'd seen in my family of origin, but fortunately I don't have the alcoholic gene. I sat outside and drank bourbon to get to sleep, sometimes taking potshots at the wild-dog packs with a BB gun. The others in Z Community couldn't see me from the main house, and I hid the bottles from the kids—just like Mom.

I kept my feelings strictly inside, not even sharing them with my best friend Neil. Moving out of the 16-person communal house helped me isolate myself. As for Jean, she was aware that I was hurting but didn't know how to talk about it with me.

I can't put it all together rationally—this whole period is just a stream of moments and feelings. It was like "the swamps of Florida" all over again. I knew I was going off the deep end, just completely burned-out. There were so many pressures about how to keep Exodus going . . . it felt like everything came down on me all at once. I couldn't take the pain anymore. All the stress from the '60s had never been released, and it was as though my system was clogged. I couldn't feel one more feeling. I'd buried that stuff, and it was coming back to get me.

I went by myself one night to see *Rocky*. Jean didn't want to see a movie about boxing, and I preferred to be alone anyway. Driving home to Grant Park, I had to pull the car off the road because I was weeping so hard. The story really got to me, got right into my soul—there was Rocky all bloody in the ring, not able to take one more punch, yet he got up again. I loved the way he kept his eyes on the prize, but he took such a beating and didn't care about how much it hurt. It seemed as though I could feel every one of my own stresses, fears, and losses of the past 15 years. How many more punches could *I* take?

Finally I called Keith Miller, a wonderful guy I'd met through Faith at Work, and I said, "I'm in trouble."

He said, "Come." He was on retreat at his beach place on the Texas Gulf Coast and had just happened to plug in his phone when I called.

Why Keith? I can't fully explain it, but he was someone I could be totally honest with. Keith was a former oilman who'd gone on to become one of the most influential lay theologians of the era. His book *The Taste of New Wine* made a huge impact on millions of people, and it's still in print today. Keith also got a degree in counseling and became a practicing psychotherapist. So he had spiritual and psychological understanding, both of which I badly needed. Also, he lived far enough away that I could unburden myself to him and then not have to see him every day.

I stayed with Keith for three or four days, just the two of us. When I arrived, he took a look at me and said, "You can talk to me about anything you want—but first go to bed." So the first two days I spent sleeping.

When I awoke, we walked the beaches for hours while I kept saying, "You just don't understand. Nobody understands. I've talked to therapists and when I get done, *they* need to be hospitalized—they can't take the intensity of what I've been through."

Keith listened to it all. He was very direct, a true no-bullshit person, and he could pull stuff out of me. He prayed with me and shared his own hurt and vulnerability, too. I woke up to the fact that people wanted to help me even if they *didn't* understand. There was enough love for me, if only I would be patient.

"I don't trust anybody," I said to Keith. "Those kids I work with— they can *feel* that I don't even trust them."

Keith said, "It doesn't matter. Of course they know that you have trouble trusting them. But you show up anyway. You keep loving them. Love is much more important than trust."

What finally got to me and turned my depression around was the way Keith kept focusing on my strengths and helping me to see my potential, my goodness. I remember him saying, "You have repressed dreams. Don't be afraid to go inside."

Even though I wasn't sure exactly what he meant, the words resonated. Today, I think I hear his message loud and clear: "Love yourself just as much as you try to love others. Go inside because the inner healing journey is also God's work."

Keith was so good at being a conduit for the holy. He just plain loved me. He spoke only words of encouragement. And by the grace of God, I picked myself up and walked on.

CHAPTER SIX

YOU COULDN'T PLAN THIS

"Six years ago, Bill Milliken was scrounging for crumbs to keep a single storefront school functioning in Atlanta. Now he is designing a prototype national program from an office next door to the White House and addressing officials of America's top corporations, invited to hear his ideas by the wife of the President and the director of the Office of Management and Budget," wrote *Washington Post* columnist David S. Broder in July 1977.

What he said was true (although "scrounging for crumbs" is a little harsh), and the story of how our tiny educational experiment in Atlanta became a national movement is frankly incredible. I wouldn't believe it myself if I hadn't lived through it, and recognized yet again how divine synchronicity can shape all our lives.

A reporter once asked me, "How did someone like you manage to get this complicated program off the ground?" There was a definite edge to her question. I could tell that she didn't have much respect for "someone like me"—undereducated, grassroots, and rather naïve politically—so I let myself get a little sarcastic in my reply.

"Well, I'm the smartest man in the world, you see," I told her. "I moved to New York City in 1960 because I knew that our Young Life urban youth clubs would give birth to Street Academies there. I knew that Wall Street CEOs would want to fund us as a response to the race riots that I could foresee would rock the city eight years later. Then I moved my family down to Atlanta in the '70s because I figured the newly elected governor—a peanut farmer with an engineering background—would probably be interested in supporting our work with poor children. Next, my colleagues and I wrote a five-year plan based on our belief that the governor would decide to run for President and win. And of course he'd take us with him to start a national program. That's all it took—sheer intelligence and foresight."

How did it really happen? I've often reflected on the unlikely combination of events that all came together in Georgia in the mid-'70s. This is where the rearview mirror really comes in handy. Living through events like these, I just scratched my head and chalked it up to coincidence or divine providence. I believe that God's grace was responsible for a lot of our successes, but I can also see patterns that weren't visible to me at the time.

Was it a coincidence that Neil and I came to Atlanta? No, we came because of Clarence Jordan's Koinonia Farm, and because Dave Lewis and his team were operating successful Street Academies there. Well, but wasn't it a coincidence that the governor of Georgia just happened to like our program? Not really. Jimmy Carter knew Clarence Jordan—after all, they were both peanut farmers—and knew all about Koinonia. The governor was a progressive Christian with a strong concern for the poor, and his values were very much shaped by Clarence and others like him. His right-hand man and later White House chief of staff, Hamilton Jordan, was Clarence's nephew.

So it's no surprise at all that Jimmy Carter responded to a couple of crazy dreamers like Neil and me. He had the same dream, nurtured in part by the same man who so influenced us. And just to round it out, one of the important offshoots of Koinonia was a program devoted to building "simple, decent, and affordable" housing, constructed by volunteer labor and sold at no profit. The program was founded in Americus, Georgia, by Millard Fuller, based on his experiences with Clarence at Koinonia. This is, of course, Habitat for Humanity, and it has remained a huge focus of Jimmy Carter's time and support.

Georgia was simply fertile soil in the 1970s, and it grew a governor who was ready to champion the needs of underserved children.

BY 1974, NEIL SHORTHOUSE, DAVE LEWIS, AND I were convinced we had a model that could reach children with needed resources and prevent them from dropping out of school. By another great stroke of grace, we persuaded Clark Jones to move down to Atlanta with his wife and kids and work with us. Our prototype was ready for replication; all we needed was state-level support. If only there were some way to meet with Georgia's new governor, Jimmy Carter. We'd heard great things about him and knew about his deep commitment to the poor. By God's grace, we voiced this desire one evening to a man who could actually do something about it.

Dr. Wayne Smith was a minister who'd become interested in our attempts to create an intentional community and had broken bread with us a number of times. Wayne was also the new governor's liaison with several communities in South America as part of a plan to create "sister city" relationships with municipalities in Georgia. (Wayne had been a missionary in São Paulo, Brazil.)

So during a meal at Z Community, he listened to our frustrations about expanding our work in Georgia, and said, "All right, I'll get you a meeting with the governor on two conditions: You can only have 20 minutes, and you have to promise not to embarrass me." We were from the streets, and we looked and acted it. Wayne was understandably worried about how we'd relate to a powerful man who also happened to be his friend.

Neil and I showed up at the governor's office bright and early one morning. Many years later, when the Carters had become our friends, President Carter told me about the first impression we made on him: "These two scraggly-looking guys came into my office, and I had to turn to my state trooper and say, 'Are these the people who are supposed to help the school system? They look like *they* need help.'"

The governor was polite to us but clearly didn't want his time wasted. In the nicest possible way, he looked at us and asked, "What do you want?"

We answered, "We need resources to replicate what we're doing with kids here in Atlanta." The governor said nothing, but made a gesture that invited us to go on. So we gave him a brief explanation of our commitment to young people and our strategies and goals.

We were astonished when he nodded and said, "All right. Let me see what I can do."

We'd managed to intrigue Carter in two ways that were extremely important to him. He could hear the passion we had for children who were falling through the cracks, and he had the same feelings. Furthermore, as we later learned, our program appealed to his intellectual side because he could see that we'd thought about the principles and had a replicable way to address the dropout problem.

Not long after that initial visit, I was presenting at a conference, and one of the other speakers was the late Ruth Stapleton, Jimmy Carter's sister. We hit it off, and she said, "The next time I'm in Atlanta, I'd like to have dinner and hear more about your work."

So when she and her husband came to town, they took me and Jean out for dinner, and then Ruth said, "Let's go back to my brother's place and hang out with them."

When we arrived at the governor's mansion, Carter was sitting on the couch, reading. He remembered me and was friendly, then excused himself and went into his study to keep working. But Rosalynn Carter was there, too, and she stayed up half the night talking to us. She really seemed to understand the concept of what we were trying to do. In fact, it was Rosalynn who eventually gave us the name "Cities In Schools," which we operated under until 1995, when the name was changed to Communities In Schools.

"Oh, I get it," she said. "You take public services and relocate them for children. You bring the cities *into* the schools. You should call it that, instead of Institutional Development Corporation." She was surely right about that.

With Rosalynn's support a major factor, we received $5,000 from the governor's emergency fund and a letter of endorsement from him that opened the door for us to raise the then-unbelievable sum of $100,000 from Atlanta leaders. We were finally being given the opportunity to prove we could really "replicate smallness on a large scale" by expanding our work to other Georgia communities.

ABOUT THIS TIME, IN EARLY 1975, I made my first visit to the White House. President Ford's chief of staff invited me after he and I had both been honored as members of "America's Ten Outstanding Young Men" by the U.S. Junior Chamber (Jaycees). When I got the telegram saying that I'd been chosen for this award, I threw it away. One of my prankster friends was clearly messing with me.

But Jean fished it out of the trash and said, "No, this is real—and you need a tuxedo, because we're going."

The commune voted to pay for the tux rental, and the Jaycees paid my plane fare to Baltimore, where the awards ceremony was. The whole thing was surreal—sitting in a banquet hall with people like Knicks basketball star (and future New Jersey Senator) Bill Bradley and the White House chief of staff, whose name was Dick Cheney.

Cheney and I hit it off. He liked what I had to say and believed that the coordination of social services was a classic conservative strategy. And it's important to state here that true political conservatives have always supported us, from the Academies all the way through the founding of Cities In Schools. One of our best friends in public life was, and is, Republican Senator Richard Lugar, who said we were "a perfect urban program" for Republicans to espouse. We're a genuinely bipartisan movement, because our two big concepts—focusing on children and integrating the delivery of needed services—transcend party politics. They make sense to *everyone*.

So Dick Cheney hated all the waste and duplication in social services, from the federal government on down. Moreover, he knew about the Street Academies from his tenure at the Office of Economic Opportunity. The upshot was that he invited me to come see him if I was ever in Washington. So I did—and walked into another moment of divine synchronicity.

After a very fruitful discussion, and a short visit to introduce myself to President Ford at Cheney's request, I was leaving the West Wing when I heard a familiar voice coming from down the hall. It was my old friend and Street Academy colleague, Dean Overman. I knocked on his door and startled the hell out of him. I was almost sure that I could tell what he was thinking: *The White House is a very secure facility. How did Bill Milliken get in here?*

"What are you doing here?" Dean asked.

"What are *you* doing here?" I replied.

Dean explained that he was now a White House Fellow. I told him about my connection with Dick Cheney, then sat down and tried to bring Dean up to date about our work in Atlanta and our ideas to replicate the new "inside the system" prototype.

Dean is one of the most intelligent people I've ever met, so if *he* doesn't understand something, there's a problem with the explanation —which there was. I kept trying to find the right metaphor and failing. But Dean just said, "Look, I can tell this is important to you, even if I don't get it. Keep in touch—you know where to find me."

JIMMY AND ROSALYNN CARTER'S SUPPORT in Georgia was amazing enough, but the next thing that happened can't be explained rationally, even looking in my rearview mirror.

Governor Carter *did* run for President in the 1976 election, and he won.

When one of our board members told me that the governor planned to announce that he was running for President, I said, "President of what?" And while I was completely supportive of his campaign, I couldn't conceal my skepticism. Was it really possible that an unknown first-term governor of a Southern state could win the Democratic nomination? And then defeat the incumbent President? A year later, all this had come to pass.

After he won, the President-elect and Rosalynn asked me to come down to their home in Plains, where Carter was interviewing people for cabinet positions.

"Hey, Bill, he wants you for Secretary of Defense," Neil insisted.

It turned out that he wanted to ask how he could help us achieve our dreams of a national program. Rosalynn had continued to champion our work, and now he was in a position to help.

I said, "Please, just help us get funding from the public and private sectors—we're ready to go. We know how to partner with the school system and help create support for the students who aren't making it. There needs to be a bridge between the schools and the community—and that's us."

Coming out of that meeting, I saw a line of reporters and photographers yelling questions at everyone who emerged from the Plains house. They saw me and kind of scratched their heads. Nobody could figure out who I was, and judging from my "grassroots" looks, obviously I wasn't going to be in the cabinet.

It got even more confusing when I walked down the steps to the driveway and saw Millard Fuller and some other Koinonia folks protesting in front of the house. They liked and respected Jimmy Carter but wanted to make their position clear from the start: "No more wars! Get rid of nuclear weapons!"

I went over and hugged everybody—it was like a family reunion. Then Neil grabbed me and got me into the car. "Are you nuts?" he asked. "You can't come out of a meeting with the President and start hugging the protesters!"

DEAN OVERMAN AND I HAD INDEED kept in touch, and after Jimmy Carter was elected, I called Dean in December of 1976 and said that I needed a place to stay in Washington. President Ford had asked Dean to continue at the White House after his fellowship and assist with the transition, even though Dean was technically now a leading partner of the prestigious law firm Winston & Strawn's Washington office.

The President-elect had asked me to write out a formal plan for exactly how we'd replicate our work, if we had the funding. "You have to give me something in writing," he kept saying. "I like what you're saying, but I have to be able to show it to other people when you're not around."

I promised that I would, well aware that putting a linear A-to-B-to-C plan down in words wasn't my strong suit. So I told Dean, "Look, I've become friends with Jimmy Carter and his family, and they want me to write up this replication idea, but I don't even know how to start. Could you help? Could that be part of your 'facilitating the transition'?"

I didn't realize this, but one of the things that happens when a new administration comes in is that everyone says, "Oh yeah, I know the new President, we're great friends." Therefore, Dean took all this with a grain of salt, but was kind enough to let me stay several times with him and his wife Linda in their Georgetown home.

One morning when I was out, Dean got a call from the "Plains, Georgia, White House switchboard" asking for me. He said I wasn't there, and the operator told him, "Please ask Bill to call Jimmy Carter at this number." So Dean decided I really did know the Carters, and he got himself assigned to help us write our paper for the new President, with approval from the outgoing Ford administration and from Winston & Strawn.

Soon it became clear that I'd need to be in Washington on a regular basis in order to work with Dean and other contacts recommended by the Carters. Jean was deep in her studies at the Candler School of Theology at Emory University, but reluctantly supported the idea of a "commuter marriage" that would take me to Washington during the week, then back to Atlanta on weekends. We knew it would be difficult, but neither of us was willing to uproot our lives yet again.

The first time I went up from Atlanta was to celebrate the inauguration. I also attended the National Prayer Breakfast, which since the Eisenhower administration had always been held right after the inauguration. There must have been thousands of people at the breakfast, but as luck would have it, my table was near the front of the room, and from my seat I was visible to Rosalynn up on the dais. After the breakfast I got a message to please call her.

I'd been wondering how to follow up with the Carters in Washington, so I was excited to respond to Rosalynn—until I realized that I had no idea how to call a First Lady. Was I supposed to find a pay phone, dial the White House, and say, "The First Lady, please"? I couldn't think of a better idea, so that was what I did. And she came right on the line and asked me if I was free to come over for lunch, since our mutual friend Wayne Smith was also there.

At the White House lunch, Rosalynn reaffirmed her intention to support our work. The atmosphere was totally informal, and I relaxed enough to be honest when she asked me about my plans, admitting that I wasn't sure where I was staying the night. She said in that warm way of hers, "Oh, why don't you just stay with us?"

So that night I called my mother in Pittsburgh and said, "Guess where I'm calling from? The Lincoln bedroom!" Even at the age of 37, a part of me still wanted to prove that my parents' low expectations of me were wrong.

Rosalynn was as good as her word, telling the press that Project Propinquity (yet another name we tried out) was her favorite program. And President Carter urged me to meet with his new Secretary of Health, Education, and Welfare (the department that's now Health and Human Services), Joseph A. Califano, Jr., to begin laying out our ideas for interagency support.

President Carter and Rosalynn let me use space in the Old Executive Office Building (OEOB) whenever I was in town. I had a title, too—Advisor on Youth Issues—but no salary. I even had a place to stay whenever I needed it. Washington hotels were not something I could easily afford, so I slept at the White House quite a bit over the next months—not in the Lincoln Bedroom, but in the family quarters, on the floor above where the President and Rosalynn had their bedroom.

They also had a little kitchen on the same floor, and one time I got thirsty during the night, so I walked downstairs and swiped a soda from their fridge. The next day, there was a note on my pillow from a staffer: "The President would prefer that you not raid his refrigerator, and we politely request that you stay on your own floor, too."

AT THE OEOB, I WAS WORKING ON the document the President had requested, with the help of Dean, Wib Walling, and Landrum Bolling, former president of the Lilly Endowment and now the head of the Council on Foundations. Landrum had been a huge supporter, first of the Street Academies and then of our move "inside the system," securing funding for us through the Lilly Endowment during his tenure there in order to back prototypes in Indianapolis and Atlanta. At this time, he volunteered to help us commit the plan to writing. It was an unusual sight, to say the least: There was the head of one of Washington's most prominent law firms, researching budget documents for us, while one of the biggest names in philanthropy sat at an old typewriter and tried to interpret my handwriting.

We sent Rosalynn memos on our progress every week to make sure she was up to date on our emerging proposal. She remained a wonderful and dedicated friend, opening doors for us in the new administration. In that *Washington Post* article, she told Broder, "I have asked the department heads to see Bill because I think what he's doing is so important. We spend money, money, money on these problems, and so many of the services are fragmented and don't even reach the people who need them."

Harv Oostdyk and a number of other Street Academy–movement colleagues spent what seemed like endless days with us on mini-retreats and planning sessions, trying to figure out how to launch a national organization that would stay true to our principles and still be able to affect the dropout problem nationwide. Burt Chamberlin, head trainer for the Postal Street Academies, was also a key member of our little brain trust. We'd rent a motel room and just hole up there, talking all night.

We realized that we needed to create an independent national board of directors that would still carry weight with educators. By serving on our board in Atlanta, Dr. Crim greatly added to our credibility, and we wanted other school superintendents to offer similar support at the national level. Our challenge was to build a structure that would last, that could survive changes in administrations and economic climate. What roles would each of us take? How could we pay everyone?

In the end, we decided that Neil would continue to refine the Atlanta prototype and expand to new locations in Georgia, while Harv developed Indianapolis and I headed the new national office. Neil and Harv clearly felt that I was the one best suited to take our collective experience to Washington, D.C. It was all about bridge building again, trying to connect the world of hurting children with the realm of federal power.

Our paper, which became known among us as "the Blue Book," was given to Carter in March, and he approved it. Rosalynn and budget director Bert Lance sponsored a breakfast for more than 200 corporate and foundation leaders at which I made the case for our new program.

Bob Baldwin at Morgan Stanley came through for us once again. He agreed to serve as a founding member of the national board, along with George Johnson and Dean Overman, who finally went to work full-time for Winston & Strawn but stayed in close touch. Members of our board met nearly every week, trying to figure out how to get the organization on a solid financial basis. For the next 20 years, I continually heard that horrible phrase *cash-flow problem,* which really means, "You're in debt!"

Bob's role was crucial: He made it clear that while he respected our passion and vision, we had a long way to go in learning how to run a business—caring wasn't enough. I know we tried his patience. Many times during those first years, the phone rang, my assistant picked it up, and I could hear Bob's voice all the way across the room: "Let me talk to Milliken!" Each time I got on the line, Bob launched right in. "Bill, you have a happy way of spending more money than you have. You're passionate, you believe in the kids, but you're disorganized as hell!"

We'd come up with one idea to garner support or funding and chase it down, then try another, then another. Bob was probably the first person who showed me what money *was,* and why you couldn't spend it if you didn't have it—unless you wanted to go out of business. Bob insisted that we become professionals, and although it took us a long time to accomplish this, I'll always be grateful to him for setting the standard. But our styles, and abilities, were so different that we became known around Washington and New York as "the Odd Couple."

A few months after we turned in the Blue Book, we got some great news: The Carter administration had located $2.7 million in federal funds to expand our prototype in Houston; Washington; New York City; and West Palm Beach, Florida. The challenge was that these funds would come from seven different federal departments. This was what we'd hoped for, as we wanted to champion cooperation and service integration from the very highest federal levels down to the individual schools and communities. But it would require a degree of coordination at the federal level that was new to me and, frankly, new to a number of the departments as well.

Dean Overman and I met regularly at Winston & Strawn, trying to figure out how to solve some very difficult bureaucratic challenges. All the federal departments had their own vested interests, and they really didn't want to integrate at the state and local level. We worked hard together for about six months. We held a lot of the meetings at Dean's office, which was right across the street from the White House. Then I'd go spend the night in a guest bedroom at the Carters' place.

Somehow I managed to be with my family in Atlanta, too. Jean was about to be ordained as an Episcopal priest. Sean, long recovered from his accident, hung out at the local Boys Club and excelled at every sport he tried. Lani was in school and was starting to experience the realities of being a mixed-race child. She didn't quite fit in, and it hurt her. Although very smart in some ways, she had a difficult time in school . . . and man, did I ever identify with that. It would take Jean, Lani, and me many years before we finally understood the true nature of the challenges she faced.

BECAUSE OF THE GRACIOUSNESS AND AFFIRMATION shown to me by the Carters, I found it easy to overlook the profound transition I was making. Jimmy and Rosalynn were genuinely "just folks" who shared many of my values—but they were also the First Family, and James Earl Carter was the leader of the most powerful nation on Earth. Everything he did was scrutinized, as were all the activities of his associates. The mores of Washington society were complicated and unfamiliar to me. It didn't even occur to me that my position as an unpaid "youth advisor" who'd been given an office in the OEOB and a bedroom at the White House when I needed it might raise a few eyebrows.

The first taste I had of inside-the-Beltway spin happened when we hired the President's son Chip to work in our new office. I'd grown to like Chip very much, and it seemed perfectly natural to take him on when he expressed interest in working for us. Had he worked 40 hours a week, his salary would have amounted to the grand sum of $26,000 a year. In fact, Chip wasn't able to spend nearly that much time with us most weeks, given his other social responsibilities as the President's son.

Two months later, unfriendly newspaper stories started to appear. They had those "denying any wrongdoing" headlines: "Chip's Hiring and Carter's Aid Not Related, Employer Says." Right, so if they're not related, why write a story about it? Basically, certain journalists (and probably certain political opponents of the Carters) were implying that we'd taken Chip on as a quid pro quo for the federal support we'd received. In fact, I'd first asked Chip about working for us long before there was any hope of federal dollars. It was all nonsense to me, but the warning was clear: In Washington politics, the *appearance* of impropriety will get you just as bad headlines as any actual misstep.

Then, in September 1978, I really got slammed. The most upsetting experience of my public life started with a phone call from my brother Ken. In between bouts of hospitalization for his alcoholism, Ken continued to make (and lose) money as a Pittsburgh businessman. Now he was calling to ask me if I could help a friend of his, George Zamias, make contact with someone at the Department of Housing and Urban Development (HUD).

Zamias was a Johnstown, Pennsylvania, developer who wanted to apply for a HUD grant to build a shopping center to help revive the city after a devastating flood the previous year—the worst since the infamous disaster in 1889. HUD had solicited proposals for redevelopment projects, and applicants had to bring matching funds to the table, which Zamias was in a position to do.

I said sure. It sounded like a worthy project, and I was glad to do a favor for my brother. I met George Zamias shortly afterward and offered to put him in touch with a deputy assistant secretary I knew at HUD. Then, as I always did—and do to this day—I told Zamias about my work with children and schools. Clearly this guy had funds and connections. Would he be interested in contributing to our new organization?

Naïve, foolish, innocent—those are the three nicest words I can think of to describe my actions. Or how about *stupid?* It honestly didn't occur to me that it would look as though I was asking to be rewarded. To my mind, I was helping someone make a connection for a grant they sounded ideal for. Then I hit him up for support for my own work, not because of the previous part of the conversation, but just because I *never* ignored an opportunity to "pass the hat" for kids. Zamias said he'd be happy to consider a contribution, we said good-bye, and I never gave it another thought. When he later sent us two checks for $5,000 each, I was delighted.

On Thursday, September 21, 1978, I woke up and read the front page of the *Washington Post*. Or rather, I *looked* at it and nearly collapsed . . . because there was my picture. "Building a White House 'Connection,'" read the headline. "Carter Family Friend Interceded at HUD for Businessman."

In the reporter's story, everything I'd done came out sounding sinister and sleazy. I'd greased the wheels for Zamias to get millions in federal funding in exchange for his payoff to my organization. I read this story as the anger and shame rose up inside me. Question me on my racial stands or my politics, sure—but don't question my integrity. There's nothing more painful, and that's what they went after. It felt like Mrs. Grundy in grade school all over again, a personal attack when I felt I'd done nothing wrong, yet couldn't help experiencing the shame of the accusation.

In a strange way, my old fears about being "dumb" were also coming back to haunt me. My relational mind sees the big picture and doesn't always connect the pieces the way many others do. So I just didn't see the linear connection between *(A)* George Zamias asking for a favor, and *(B)* Bill Milliken asking him for a contribution. That had nothing to do with the big picture that I cared about, but to a Washington reporter, *A* plus *B* equaled, "Hmm, maybe he's crooked." I knew that I wasn't dishonest . . . but I *was* still afraid that I was dumb.

As it happened, I had three appointments that day: with Rosalynn Carter, Senator Ted Kennedy, and investigative journalist Jack Anderson. When I arrived at the White House to see the First Lady, the President's press secretary, Jody Powell, pulled me into his office and said, "Bill, you have to get out of here. You can't meet Mrs. Carter today." Again, in my naïveté, it hadn't occurred to me that maybe this wasn't the best morning to keep the appointment.

"Okay," I stammered, and mentioned that I was also scheduled to see Kennedy and Anderson. Maybe I should cancel them, too?

Jody gave me a look and said, "Don't you *dare* go to those meetings."

That night on the seven o'clock news, there was Walter Cronkite—Walter Cronkite!—covering the story, staring gloomily out of the TV screen. The program cut to a shot of the White House, with the camera zooming in on an ordinary-looking window. "This is the room where Bill Milliken sleeps when he comes to Washington," Cronkite intoned. It was as though I'd become a notorious criminal overnight. I wanted to pull my blanket over my head and never come out.

It got worse. My two hometowns, Pittsburgh and Atlanta, gave the story front-page coverage the next day. I was interviewed by reporters who quoted me accurately—I told them it was a mistake in judgment—yet every story made it sound like I was full of shit. Zamias was bewildered, too. He was trying to get a grant to help revive Johnstown, bringing $18 million to the table in matching funds, but he was being accused of unethical conduct.

You have to keep in mind that the Watergate scandal, which forced a President out of office, was only a few years old. Journalists were heroes, and investigative reporting was a noble, patriotic undertaking. Every reporter in Washington wanted to break a new "-gate" scandal. Carter's enemies in the press jumped all over the story.

Jody Powell, many years later, told me, "We were outsiders, too, you know, just like you. You can't believe how mean-spirited people in Washington can be. There are stories I'll never tell . . ."

In my case, they wrote op-ed pieces containing phrases such as "the sad case of Bill Milliken," "the gullibility of Carter," and "religious men who wheel and deal." I was called "an innocent," a "religious do-gooder," "sweet and trusting," and "terribly gullible." None of them dared to claim I was dishonest, but some of them tried to imply it.

For a day or two I was frozen by the fear and shame. Up till that point, nobody in Washington knew my name, and that was the way I liked it. So here was my very first national media exposure, and what was the subject? It was my failings, a scandal. I'd embarrassed myself, the Carters, and all my colleagues; and I'd probably brought our whole movement down with one thoughtless action. It was like having the worst parts of my self-image suddenly out there on the front page for everybody to see.

Finally, I went to talk to Dean Overman at his office. He said, "I've read this and read this, and I still can't figure out what you're supposed to have done wrong. But there are reporters staked out at the White House, and all the questions at the press briefing this morning were about you. So you need to get out of town until they find something else to write about." He drove me to Baltimore to catch a plane for Atlanta, because he said that reporters would be waiting at the Washington airports, too.

And what came of it all? Absolutely nothing. It felt as though my whole world were crashing down—the White House even promised a "probe" into "anything that appears improper"—and now it's just a blip from long ago. But it didn't seem small then. We had a big meeting in Atlanta, Neil, Dave Lewis, Dean, Harv, and I. We thought my naïveté might have cost us everything.

Harv said that we had to carry on as if the whole thing were behind us and just keep moving. He wanted me to go back and face the Carters as soon as possible. I didn't want to see them, of course. I thought I'd completely embarrassed them. A man with my street background had been welcomed and treated like family, and I repaid them by letting them down.

Finally, when I got my nerve back, I called Rosalynn. She was incredibly kind about it. All she said was, "Oh, that's the way they are."

Chip phoned me and said, "Don't worry about it. My dad called Ben Bradlee at the *The Washington Post* and said, 'This is ridiculous, there's nothing to it.'"

I don't think it was any coincidence that I heard from a *Post* journalist later that same week. He apologized to me, saying, "You obviously just don't know this town yet. It's clear you didn't understand that people will want to get close to you because you have such access to the Carters."

It seemed so hard to believe: Why would Zamias need access? What he wanted me to do, he could have done himself with a phone call. It never crossed my mind to use my precious "access" and tell any member of the Carter family about some friend of my brother's who wanted to apply for a matching HUD grant.

FOR A COUPLE OF MONTHS, THE SO-CALLED scandal did freeze our funding, public and private, and a lot of people weren't taking my calls. But the White House probe came to nothing, and there was never even a suggestion of lawbreaking, so eventually the reporters stopped writing stories, and everything returned to normal. One paper ran a couple of paragraphs (on page 17, not on page 1) saying that Carter family friend Bill Milliken had been cleared by the White House of any wrongdoing.

An op-ed piece by Hal Gulliver, an editor with the *The Atlanta Journal-Constitution,* got it about right: "This particular mini-flap will probably have an even shorter than usual life in Washington talk," he wrote a week after the story broke, "simply because there really is not anything sinister there, and the programs which Milliken has helped run may well involve a higher percentage of idealistic people trying to help the poor than anything comparable in the country."

Gulliver gave me a scolding—"Oh, it was dumb enough, if you please; the appearance of evil in a political context is often almost as serious as real evil"—and called me "naïve at the least" for putting myself "even remotely in the position of seeming to peddle influence." But he made the point that "wounded reporters," as he called them, were still disappointed not to have been part of investigating Watergate and badly wanted to uncover "current ill-will." He also called our work with young people "real and impressive," and strongly applauded the Carters for supporting us and for not backing down in the face of this event.

There was one touch of humor, anyway. I got called about a follow-up story some rag wanted to do, claiming that I was really Italian and had Mafia connections. "Is it true you got your White House perks in return for funneling dirty money into the Carter campaign?" I was tempted to dig up the Tedesco family's number and give it to them, but realized no one would be laughing.

I learned a few things from this painful episode. One was that I might be smart and experienced in some areas, yet completely naïve in others. The world of Washington politics needed to be navigated just like the streets of the Lower East Side. In some ways it was even more dangerous, because at least on the streets I knew who my enemies were. In Washington, nobody really knew me or had anything personal against me. It was all guilt by association. Jimmy Carter and the members of his administration were the ones with enemies.

So my 15 minutes of notoriety was another lesson in humility, which I believe means understanding my place in life. With my background, being humble came pretty naturally. What had I studied? What was my career? I knew how to hang out, and I cared about young people. All I ever tried to do was to stay focused on the kids and on love.

"Love your neighbor as yourself"—sometimes it seems that we human beings do everything we can not to hear that. It's so simple and so radical. But of course, we also have to find ways to live it out, to be "wise as serpents and harmless as doves," as Scripture puts it. That kind of wisdom was something I needed to learn, when it came to the ways of Washington.

Then there was the whole question of influence, which I hadn't even realized I possessed. I didn't think of myself as a person in any position of power. But I was. Knowing the First Family, having that "access," I was envied by a lot of people. I was coming from a culture of sharing and generosity—not only regarding material things but in evaluating people's motives—and I'd run up against the Washington subculture of competition and distrust.

I didn't exercise the least bit of influence on behalf of George Zamias, but the point is that I *could* have tried to, so some people assumed that I did. Appearances count for so much, and it *looked* bad. This woke me up to a more realistic understanding of my position as the head of a national organization. The more leadership I tried to offer, the more people I built relationships with, the more favors were asked of me. And they weren't always requests that ought to be granted.

This is the difficult part of basing success on personal relationships: they have a cost, too. Much as I cared about others, I had to learn how to say, "No." Mainly, I've gotten smarter about knowing

144

when *not* to use what influence I possess. Young people building their own movements need to know this, too: Anything that looks like self-gain or self-promotion has to be rejected out of hand. And I emphasize "*looks* like."

The other great lesson was this: I found out who my friends were, who really loved me and would stand by me. George Johnson, Landrum Bolling, Dean Overman, Anne Cox Chambers, and Jimmy and Rosalynn Carter all rallied around. So did the Z Community down in Atlanta, and of course my beloved family. George made a great point, saying, "The minute I read those stories, I knew they weren't true, because I know *you*. But just think how readily we believe the same garbage if it's about people we don't know and don't like."

Everyone surrounded me with love. I was frozen, with all my feelings hidden away. The community thawed me out and helped me get my voice back. At first they all kind of walked around me, giving me some space. I just wanted to hide in a corner. I was thinking, *I don't give a shit what happens next.* I'd thought I was a leader, and look what I'd done.

And of course my pride was wounded. I was so good on the streets, but I'd flunked Washington 101. So having my community and family hanging tight with me, being patient, and helping me to know they loved me, was the healing I needed. Sometimes a really awful episode can provide the opportunity to understand and take in how much we matter to others.

I realize, too, that with the passage of time, all the allegations and headlines just don't matter anymore. And really, they didn't mean much at the time either. So I suppose that's another lesson: It's so easy to overreact, to think the world is coming to an end, when this kind of adversity hits. How could I not take it personally? But it's not personal at all. Politics, especially, is always going to be painful. I tried to be more thick-skinned, but a person would have to be really insensitive not to feel it when his name is smeared.

I was staying in the White House guest bedroom one night in 1979 when Jean called. "Guess what," she said dully. "The house got broken into again. This time, instead of breaking a window, they took the front door off with a crowbar. I found all my personal things dumped on the floor. Don't worry, we're all fine, and there wasn't much to steal, as you know."

I started to commiserate with her when she interrupted me.

"And there you are, safe and secure at the White House. You know what? *That's not fair.*"

She was right, and the point got even clearer when I returned that weekend. Sure enough, no front door, and when I walked into the kitchen to make a cup of coffee, I saw something long, pink, and hairless hanging out of the napkin drawer.

"Jean!" I screamed. "What the hell is that?"

She stood with her arms folded, smiling sweetly at me. "Oh, that, dear? That's a dead rat. The kids and I found it there yesterday. We decided we'd leave it for you to deal with."

I got the message: Something had to change. Much as I loved our Atlanta community, I wasn't spending much time there. Jean wanted a safer place for herself and the children, and better public schools. She was almost finished with her two-year residency in pastoral psychotherapy at Georgia Baptist Hospital and would soon be free to move. And our new Cities In Schools program needed a real office in Washington.

Jean said, "We're only going to D.C. if it's a decent neighborhood—no more robberies and rats."

I agreed with her on that one. With Neil and Dave's blessing, we began to plan the move. Our prototypes in the new cities were just getting off the ground, and Neil needed to keep cultivating the Atlanta program. I would once again help spearhead the national movement from a new office in the nation's capital.

It was 1980, and within a year we were dealing with a serious setback. Our friend Jimmy Carter was back in Plains, and Ronald Reagan was the President. Cities In Schools had become "Carter's program." The '80s were about new challenges, not only for my commitment to the nation's young people, but for my own children as well.

CHAPTER SEVEN

GOING NATIONAL

Ronald Reagan left California to come to Washington, and Jean, Sean, Lani, and I left Atlanta not long afterward. We found a beautiful single-family home in North Arlington, about 15 minutes from downtown Washington.

I hadn't lived in a suburban-type community since I was a kid, and the culture shock was enormous. Also, the demographics of the neighborhood were skewed toward retirees. There were only two other families with young children. Mainly, it was a lot of retired military and foreign-service people and plenty of federal-government workers. Over the years, I watched the federal workers come and go as administrations changed.

So it was tough to put down roots. True to our word, Jean and I made sure the neighborhood was a better place to raise and school our children. Back in Atlanta, Jean had volunteered in the local elementary school when Sean entered first grade, but the public education was so bad in our neighborhood that many parents were looking for an alternative.

Our community started a cooperative school, taught largely by parents through the use of the arts, called Peachtree Alternative School, which Sean and Lani both attended. Several of the young single women in our community taught there, and Jean, having completed a B.S. in elementary education, was the natural choice for director. They charged on a sliding scale according to income.

When Sean was ready for middle school, we looked around for an affordable private school, despite the fact that it violated our commitment to public education. The options in our neighborhood were so bad. Students were falling behind one or even two grades, and we were worried that Sean would become another "failure" through no fault of his own.

Both Jean and I hated the conflict between what we believed philosophically and what we felt we had to do for our children. In the end, we decided that it was a greater wrong to deny our kids the best education we could give them, if we had the means to do so, than it was to violate our principles.

It was a tough compromise: We'd continue living in our low-income neighborhood, keep working to improve the public schools in our neighborhood, but until we reached a critical mass of families who were committed to change the quality of local education, we'd send our kids to private school. How could it be right to sacrifice our children's future by giving them an inferior foundation, when what we valued and were working for was a quality education for *all* children? It was one of those quandaries where there's no perfect answer. We made the best call we could.

Our eventual choice was Woodward Academy, a private school south of the city, and one of my board members helped us with the tuition. Sean was bused across the city for 40 minutes to attend class. Thus, his home and school communities were completely separate.

In Arlington, however, Sean and Lani could catch a school bus on the corner and be taken to public schools only a few miles away. Sean's high school was rated one of the finest in the nation, and he did very well there.

Still, it felt strange to be in suburbia. Jean and I badly needed a community to replace the one we'd had in Atlanta. Through some Young Life friends who were working in Washington and Northern Virginia, we met John Gardner and his wife, Ann, who were raising kids our children's ages. The Gardners introduced Jean to the rector of the church they attended. She was hired as a part-time assistant, and there we began to find community. The next thing we knew, we were being integrated into a larger group of like-minded people. It was the beginning of our "house church," which included the Gardners, Dean and Linda Overman, and the Hattwicks—our family doctor and his wife—and is still meeting at least once a month, almost 30 years later.

The house church didn't replace formal worship, but worked more like a support group. When we began it, we were eight people who'd been in Episcopal churches but for one reason or another hadn't found a "home" in a particular parish at the moment. Then over the years, as we all found church communities we liked, we'd go to our different churches on Sunday. But each Saturday night, we gathered at one of our homes for informal worship that often lasted several hours. Jean, as our ordained clergyperson, led the service and celebrated the Eucharist. Alternating members would teach the scriptural lesson each week, followed by a long and intense discussion of what it meant to us personally, interspersed with periods of meditation and music. And then we'd all have dinner.

Once again, the communal spirit that Jean and I had found to be so crucial for our family and spirituality was playing a vital role in our lives. And I know that the practice of shared leadership we developed was important to Jean. At the beginning, some of the women didn't have confidence in their ability to understand and interpret Scripture, but that changed, and Jean was a big part of it.

Even though our suburban home at first felt isolating and uncomfortable, it ended up being a healthier situation for me. Always, in the past, there was *no leaving.* From Harlem on, as soon as I walked out the door, there was my ministry; there was my life. The workday had no beginning or end, and there was never any refuge from it, especially at 215 Madison. While our new house was still close to downtown D.C., Jean and I had a little haven we could retreat to. It was all part of trying to take better care of myself, to shed that driven, high-intensity, street lifestyle from the '60s.

Jean said, "You don't have to answer the phone every time it rings, and now you live 15 minutes away from your work. Enjoy it!"

Before, our office was in our home, or else right in the neighborhood. The neighbors were people whose kids were in our academies, and the commune itself was often a challenging part of our journey. There was no space, no leaving.

This little 15-minute barrier between home and work made me realize something I never knew: I'm actually not an extrovert. I get very attuned to people when I speak, when there's an audience, but then I want seclusion. At a public event or party, I'm always in a corner talking with one person. I get recharged that way, by a serious conversation rather than chitchat.

Over the years, I discovered that a lot of performers—such as musicians, actors, and politicians—are introverts, too. They're friendly and love to connect, but then they need not to be "on" all the time. I'd never acknowledged those same needs in myself. Somehow I thought that I could always be on. Understanding myself better was all part of the inward journey, a way of finding the energy and spiritual direction that allowed me to then reach out and relate to others in need. It's a full circle. Too often, I've ignored my great need for introspection and the result was unhealthy physically, emotionally, and spiritually.

THE FIRST CIS NATIONAL OFFICE WAS LOCATED in the basement of Landrum Bolling's house in Georgetown. A secretary, an executive assistant, and I were crammed down there, although I have to admit that it was one of the nicest basements I've ever spent time in, being in Georgetown and everything. So before dawn, I drove over the Key Bridge from Arlington and opened up shop for the day.

We also had a local CIS program operating in Washington, D.C. The office was in a YMCA at 14th and W Streets, Northwest. Called the Adolescent Health Center, it provided food for kids, nutrition, health screenings, babysitting for young mothers, obstetric care when needed, and day care throughout the school day. The whole operation was very hands-on. The energetic and compassionate young secretary would leave her desk to take girls to doctor's appointments, or bring food to families' houses. Her name was Onita Terrell, and she now holds the record for longest (by far!) employment with CIS National at 28 years. She's also one of my dearest friends and a blessing to everyone who knows her and has worked with her.

Back in 1981, I wondered if Cities In Schools could last 28 months, much less 28 years. It looked as though the Reagan presidency might do us in. CIS was identified by the federal agencies as "Jimmy Carter's program" or "Rosalynn's pet project," and it became almost a badge of honor for bureaucrats to scorn us as liberals.

But if that were true, what was Robert H. B. Baldwin doing as chairman of our board? Why had Senator Lugar called us a "perfect" program for Republicans to support? Why would Jack Kemp point to us as "the most conservative social program in America"? CIS's approach is, in fact, very conservative about how money is spent. Furthermore, we insist that the private sector, not government, has to be the prime mover in setting up a local CIS effort.

Frankly, I think that I'm more conservative than a lot of people who give themselves that label. They don't have a plan to conserve anything, they just say, "Cut the budget." I want to stop wasting money and resources, and instead coordinate what we do have to work more efficiently and effectively, leveraging it even more.

There are unbelievable layers of duplication within government agencies—five or six different departments, whether at the federal, state, or local level, all targeting the same problem through the eyes of their respective missions. Through CIS, we show everyone a way to work together. The government can spend the same amount of money and accomplish five times as much, as long as folks don't mind sharing the credit. *That's* being conservative.

One of the first things I learned in Washington was to hate these terms anyway. You want to call me a liberal-conservative-agnostic-Christian-interfaith-middle-of-the-roader? Fine, it's not going to change what I do. I learned this from Clarence Jordan: Don't point to anyone and use labels that alienate him. The way you've chosen to act will make your enemies for you. You'll get plenty of political scorn because your life is often a testament that you don't agree with others. If your daughter is mixed race and your friends are African American and Latino, then people who don't like that will see you as part of the problem. But I didn't create that, I didn't choose my family and friends to make a political point.

SOME SKILLS DON'T TRANSFER TO NEW job descriptions. Being good on the streets doesn't always mean being a good manager. There were plenty of people who joined the CIS movement but didn't understand the fine art of compromise, for instance. One of my closest associates at the national office in the '80s eventually got so fed up and furious with the way things were going that he stormed into my office after hours, slammed the door, pulled a gun, and said, "Now shut the fuck up and listen to me!" We worked out an amicable separation shortly after that.

For me, the challenge was always to find the right people to help me. Growing up, I did well in school only if I succeeded in pulling a little team together on my behalf—one person to summarize the material for me, another to type my papers, and so on. And I found the same thing as the head of a national organization. I just couldn't do it alone as "president." Being in charge of anything still felt like a joke—the way it did when my friends got me elected vice president in high school.

It took years before I saw that these constant, irritating management problems at CIS were a sign of a deeper place where I still needed self-understanding. Asking for help and letting others take responsibility never came easy for me, and I believe our organization suffered for it.

In the first years of the Reagan presidency, Cities In Schools was always on the brink of financial failure. The one constant that kept us going was the support of Herb Alpert and Jerry Moss, co-founders of A&M Records. Herb, of course, was widely known as the trumpet-playing leader of the Tijuana Brass, which scored 14 top-40 hits in the '60s. I met Herb and Jerry in the late '70s, and the three of us became good friends. They seemed to understand exactly what I was trying to do for kids, and they both had—and still have—huge, generous hearts.

So when our funding dried up in the early '80s, Herb and Jerry said, "We'll fund 'the office of the president of CIS' so that you can keep going." And they've continued to do that to this day. But when they first began, "the office of the president" was a huge chunk of our budget, since apart from my assistant and me, there wasn't much to the CIS national office. They also opened doors for us in the California entertainment community. Our board was generous with its donations, but the fact is that without Herb and Jerry, I don't see how we could have made it.

Slowly, with many frustrating setbacks, we began to find sympathetic ears in the new Republican administration. The big turning point came in February 1985, when, thanks to Bob Baldwin, I met Barbara Bush, Vice President George H. W. Bush's wife. We had lunch together, and I couldn't swallow a bite, knowing that I had just one hour with her and that it would be my only chance to win her support. Furthermore, CIS was in desperate financial straits at that moment, so I talked nonstop while Mrs. Bush ate lunch.

When I finally paused for breath, she told me that she was very interested in what I had to share about Cities In Schools, but she'd already chosen *her* favorite program, which was about adult illiteracy.

"Well, that's perfect," I said. "That's exactly what we're all about."

"What do you mean?" she asked me. "I thought you worked with schoolchildren."

"We do," I said. "We're working to prevent adult illiteracy before it starts. Isn't that a great idea?"

Mrs. Bush laughed and said, "Okay, I get it. How can I help?"

I asked her for two things: to join us for the opening of a CIS school site in Houston and to arrange a meeting for me with Attorney General Ed Meese, one of the toughest Republicans in Washington.

A week or so later, I called Neil Shorthouse around 11 P.M. There was no big crisis—in fact, I had some good news I wanted to share. Jean and the kids were in bed, but I was wired as usual, and I knew my old buddy Neil would still be up. He was the only person I ever met who got by on less sleep than I did, and who worked longer hours. (Neil was once asked to be the head of a complicated urban development effort, and he said sure—but how many hours a week? He wasn't going to quit CIS. Well, it's 40 hours a week, he was told. "Oh, no problem," Neil assured the guy. "For me, that's part-time.")

So how were things in Atlanta? I asked. Neil filled me in on our Exodus program's accomplishments and some personal updates on the Z Community members I knew so well. And how was my life in D.C.?

"Neil," I said, "do you know who Ed Meese is?"

"Sure, Reagan's new attorney general. He wants to take away people's Miranda rights. What did he do, try to arrest you?"

"Actually . . . he's going to reinstate our federal funding through the Department of Justice."

Neil just said, "No way."

Attorney General Meese was considered a hard-core conservative, what we'd call a "cultural conservative" today. Probably he and I would have disagreed on plenty of social issues, but when it came to children, there was no conflict at all. When Mrs. Bush arranged a meeting with him, I thanked him for his time and then simply said, "If you want to make progress on juvenile delinquency, keep the kids in school. Every study ever done will tell you that. And we think CIS can help."

Ed Meese knew Bob Baldwin, and I'm guessing that along with Mrs. Bush's endorsement, that was a deciding factor. He became our champion in the government and succeeded in reinstating our federal funding through the Department of Justice, just as I told Neil. Bob then had the attorney general come and speak to some top-level business people at an event hosted at Morgan Stanley. It helped our standing in the business world a lot, as corporate leaders got the message that the dropout crisis wasn't about Democrats or Republicans— it was about *all* our children.

All along we'd been saying that stopping the flow of dropouts wasn't primarily the problem of educators. It affected so many segments of society, and it would require the participation and coordination of resources far beyond the schools. Now the Department of Justice was saying, "Yes, large percentages of dropouts become juvenile delinquents, then criminals, and then go to prison, so we're going to support a dropout-prevention program as part of our mission."

Ed Meese helped us create a funding partnership with three other federal departments, all of which saw the logic of collaborating around dropouts. The Department of Health and Human Services said, "Dropouts are a huge drain on our public-welfare system; count us in." The Department of Labor said, "Dropouts can't get decent jobs, so we want to help, too." And the Department of Education, the fourth member of what became known as the Partnership Plan, had a natural stake in the issue to begin with.

We were getting concrete proof of what we'd been saying since 1960: Keep the focus on kids, and support will come from all political parties and walks of life. We were also finding more and more ways to show what building bridges and making connections for kids can mean. The Partnership Plan is a great example. If four federal departments are going to pool their resources and cooperate around a critical national issue, someone has to stand in the middle and be the coordinator. That's what CIS does.

In the schools, we try to be invisible: We aren't another "program," but simply the means through which local resources and services can be delivered efficiently and effectively. The great composer and arranger Quincy Jones might have given us the best illustration of this process when he observed, "You're like the orchestra leader, helping everybody play their individual instruments together and make good music." It was the same thing at the federal government level: We didn't want four federal agencies to each fund a new "dropout department." Instead, we were showing them a way to coordinate the efforts they were *already* making to keep kids in school. What they needed was someone to step up and say, "Here, channel your efforts through us. We have the experience and the local connections. We'll get you the most results for every dollar you spend."

As THE '80s ROLLED ON, MY OUTWARD journey continued to surprise me. Years later, when I saw *Forrest Gump*, I recognized myself onscreen as that outsider who found himself in the same room with politicians, millionaires, and famous musicians. The inner journey, the path of healing and spiritual self-knowledge, was also filled with surprises.

Here's a big one: If it weren't for my daughter, Lani, I never would have been able to understand my own learning issues.

Jean and I had adopted Lani in 1970, when she was an infant, and we could see that she had special issues. Lani didn't sleep through the night until she was ten, and she was very slow to talk. Sometimes she had scary episodes in which she appeared to hallucinate. We knew little about her biological background. At that time in New York, that was the law—adoptive parents weren't allowed to have much information about birth families.

In addition, Lani was tri-racial—black, white, and Asian—so there was no natural community with which she could identify. Talk about stuck in the middle—Lani experienced that from day one. In Atlanta, she was bullied, and while that got better when we moved to Virginia, she still had many academic difficulties as she prepared to enter middle school. We consulted doctors and educators and became pretty sure that she'd experienced some kind of fetal drug syndrome that may have led to malnourishment or failure to thrive. She was surviving in public school but clearly needed some additional help if she was going to graduate.

Then we found out about the Lab School, an incredible institution in Washington, D.C., that teaches kindergarten through high school students with learning disabilities. They also offer testing and after-school programs, and when we started taking Lani there, the difference was apparent.

Our daughter doesn't easily take in what she hears, and she gets overloaded if she's around too many people, which made school hell. She had difficulty focusing and acted impulsively; the Lab School gave her many strategies for dealing with these issues. The whole thing was a big relief for me and Jean, too. Both of us, Jean especially, worried that we hadn't been good parents. We finally understood that the challenge was just how our daughter's brain worked.

This was also the first time I truly acknowledged my own learning issues. I'd never been direct about it before, never talked openly to a professional about that feeling of "being dumb" that had haunted me since I was a child. But the head of the Lab School immediately saw the signs in me when she interviewed us and Lani. She asked me a bunch of questions about my history and then asked, "So were you ever diagnosed with a learning disability?"

The Lab School director talked to me a lot about my learning style. This was when I first learned about *imprinting* and discovered that my mind doesn't retain written words in the typical way. I thought about Mrs. Grundy back in grade school, humiliating me in front of the class because I told her that I couldn't remember what I'd just read. At last, it was all clear to me.

I was also finally able to see that my brain is just wired differently, and that there are benefits to it, as well as challenges. It's as if I have four or five televisions turned on in my head at the same time. When I don't seem to be listening, Jean will ask, "Where are you?" and I'll say, "Uh, channel 22?"

The inside of my head is a busy place, and I don't have many controls, although I've learned how to handle it much better over the years. There's a lot of film all the time, and new images are constantly being generated. For instance, I watched the news about Hurricane Katrina, and in my mind I saw a ship going down, even though that wasn't being shown on the screen. I concentrated on this picture and realized it had a whole story for me: The "haves," the people with money and position, made it off the sinking ship because they could afford upper berths and deck chairs and could get to the lifeboats quickly. Why did my brain create that picture? I have no idea; maybe I made a connection with the *Titanic*. I just automatically think in illustrations and metaphors.

Then another part of my brain showed me a picture of musicians with guitars, and I realized, *Oh, they're going to have rallies and fund-raising events for the hurricane victims.* I make connections very fast and put them together in a picture. The cameras are all going at once; the downside is that sometimes the words get left way behind. I also tend to leap from a fresh idea, full of passion, to the vision of the end product, forgetting that there are usually a lot of process steps in between.

I've even come to terms with some of the small, funny things my brain does. I always know when somebody's approaching behind me. I can sense people in the room, and I can pick up on their moods instantly. I'm hypersensitive to the energy in a room. I think this started in fear—for years, I wouldn't sit with my back to the door, as I mentioned earlier—but now I can just feel it.

Sometimes I can't listen to music because it distracts me; I can't think. Music is very creative, always going off on its own thing—and I'm trying to do that, too, so it gets in the way. If I were more linear, maybe music would help me get away from that, but it's as though we're competing in the right brain, where I live. The music collides with my ideas.

Jean will say, "Let's put on the radio" while we're driving, and I'll say, "No, I'm thinking."

Today, it's all a source of wonder to realize how different and amazing we humans are. The brain is always looking for ideas and solutions; it's such a creative place. If we're faced with a linear problem and can't solve it, *A* to *B* to *C,* then it may be tempting to give up because the left brain is of no use. So I've learned to encourage that switch over to the other side, where I'm more comfortable and my cognition is more developed. Then I'll realize, *Okay, there are multiple solutions.*

At the same time, I've worked to expand and appreciate my left-brain skills—which really do exist, despite a lot of the kidding I've gotten over the years. My mind can achieve more than I ever gave it credit for, it turns out. I have no trouble thinking conceptually or following abstract reasoning. That's not the same as "thinking linearly," which I've never been good at and never will be.

As for Lani, we knew she was smart, yet didn't see how she could handle college. But the Lab School helped her identify a college in West Virginia that would meet her needs. She made it through—not easily, but with tremendous commitment, determination, and good grades—and decided to become a nurse after graduating with her B.A.

It was just astonishing; I couldn't have passed any of the tests that she did. During Lani's clinical work, she learned that hospital nursing required abilities that didn't come quickly enough for her to keep up with that fast-paced, high-pressure setting. But she found that as a registered nurse, she's great with patients one-on-one. So now she's a home-care skilled nurse, taking the most difficult cases, and her patients and their families love her. She definitely has the gift of creating a healing environment.

When Lani was in her early 20s, she decided that she wanted to find out whatever she could about her biological parents. Jean thought this was great since she herself had grown up not knowing her biological father. She knew who he was and heard stories about him because he lived in Pittsburgh, too, but there was no contact until Jean was a young woman. Then she took the initiative and got in touch with him, visited him, and met his second wife and kids. It ended up being a really important thing to do for her identity and peace of mind. So although Jean never pushed Lani to learn about her birth parents, when our daughter was ready, Jean supported her strongly.

Lani didn't know anything. All we'd ever been able to tell her was that she was black, white, and Filipina, and that her parents were married but not able to care for her. At her initiative, we went with her to meet with staff at the adoption agency. They provided a little more information that enabled her to do a search and find that her birth records were there in New York City.

The surname was unusual, so Lani was able to continue the search using phone directories. If it had been Smith or Jones, the whole thing would have ended right there. Lani called one family who said, "It's not us, but we think we know which family this might be." Using their information, Lani went to the public library and looked up the obituary of the person who turned out to be her grandfather. From there, she got the names of his children and finally made contact with her family of origin.

Their story wasn't a happy one. Lani was the youngest of four children. All three of her older siblings had been either adopted by family members or placed in foster care—her biological parents were simply unable to care for children. Her oldest sister, for example, was adopted by an aunt who was a pediatrician. Lani discovered that her mother received heavy drugs in a mental hospital, then got pregnant shortly after her discharge and gave birth to Lani in her early 40s. The birth was kept secret, Lani was given up for adoption, and the rest of the family didn't even know she existed.

Lani learned from her grandfather's obituary that he was a professor of biochemistry at the University of Pennsylvania with a Ph.D. in philosophy from New York University. The entire family worked in science or medicine. But Lani's father probably also had severe learning disabilities. He ended up as a janitor, then killed a guy in a barroom fight and went to prison, where he died shortly before Lani learned all this. One of her sisters lived on the streets during adolescence, and a brother who suffered from mental illness had disappeared. As for Lani's mother, she was back in a mental hospital when Lani traced her and died of cancer just a few months before Lani tried to see her.

So the evidence of heredity is very convincing, and not just in the areas of learning or social difficulties. Lani graduated from college and felt called to be a nurse, although no one in our family had anything to do with the medical field. At this time, she had no knowledge of any of the medical and scientific background of her grandfather and his family. Yet two of her sisters became nurses, and two aunts were doctors. Also, Lani is a natural artist, and she found out that her father was also a gifted artist, who learned to paint while in prison.

For the first time, Lani felt as though she understood who she was, even if the truth was painful. I remember her hugging Jean and me, saying, "I always felt like I was dropped from the sky, but now I feel that I belong here because I know where I came from."

She'd never understood why her mother gave her up, but knowing so much more about her family of origin, Lani could accept that mental illness made her mother unfit to parent her.

Lani also made a deeper commitment to our family as a result of this episode. Often, adopted girls tend to believe they're "abandoned princesses" who came from great wealth, or else from a noble but poor mother who couldn't take care of them. They make up all these fantasies, thinking, *Maybe I would have been happier if I were never adopted!* Lani finally knew the truth, and she realized that it wouldn't have been a good situation if she'd stayed with her birth family.

The best thing about our whole experience with Lani and the Lab School, where this part of the journey began, was finding out that we weren't alone. There are so many children who learn differently, and so many learning-disability support networks out there. A lot of the most powerful people in Washington have kids with similar issues. Of all the awards I've been given, the one I'm proudest of came from the Lab School in 2009. They recognize three "Outstanding Achievers with Learning Disabilities" annually, and that year I was one of them.

Again, this was all divine synchronicity. God gave me a special gift by bringing Lani into our family: In seeking to provide for her needs, *I* began to heal. I only wish it hadn't taken me so many years to under-stand and accept myself. But in thousands of schools, organizations such as CIS are reaching out to kids who learn differently, taking away the stigma of "being dumb."

CIS GREW STEADILY THROUGH THE 1980s and '90s. We continued to benefit from Clark Jones's commitment to children and to us. He made the move to Washington and played a variety of key roles for CIS. He started our first regional office in the Southeast and later over-saw our entire five-region network of CIS affiliates. Other dedicated and talented colleagues gave us a level of professionalism that was both welcome and new. Peter Bankson, for instance, came to us after nearly 30 years in the Army and helped forge important partnerships with the Department of Defense and several other federal agencies.

If you want to learn more about the Communities In Schools story, you can read many of the important milestones in my book *The Last Dropout*. We were supported by each successive administration, although I was never in anyone's inner circle, not even the Carters. I didn't get invited to high-level meetings. As a bridge builder, a con-nector, I didn't worry about being part of the inner circle.

As far as Washington went, I was in it but not of it—no different from hanging out on the streets with gang members, really. In fact, I was more afraid and isolated living and working in Washington than I ever was in Harlem. It felt claustrophobic, and it often made me ner-vous. I just wanted to get the job done and go home. Being a mover and shaker isn't one of my gifts. In some respects, that's hurt CIS, be-cause I strongly resisted being a public figure. When the Bridgespan Group helped us create a strategic plan in the mid-2000s, they said, "CIS is the best-kept secret in the U.S." I know part of the reason is that I hate doing talk shows and media interviews and trying to be-come a high-profile spokesperson as a way of helping CIS.

Still, I crossed paths with a lot of well-known people. There was a day in June 1983 when I got a call from businessman and philan-thropist Maurice Tempelsman. He'd been a generous supporter of our work, but I'd never had a personal phone call from him before. He asked if I could visit him in New York to meet a friend of his who was concerned about what her son was going to do after college. I said sure, wondering what was so important.

Tempelsman had a beautiful, ornate office, full of antique furniture and art, and one wall covered by a huge map of the world. I walked in for our meeting, greeted him, and saw a woman sitting at the table with her back to me. She turned around and said, "Hi, I'm Jackie."

I said, "Oh. And your son must be John."

I couldn't believe I was talking to Jackie Onassis. At that time, I didn't know of her relationship with Tempelsman, so I was totally surprised and nervous. But after a few minutes, I saw that she was like any other mother—concerned about her son. In her soft-spoken, engaging manner, she explained that John wasn't sure what he wanted to do after graduating from Brown, and she wondered if we had any internships.

Even though we didn't, I said, "You bet!"

We created an internship opportunity for John Kennedy, Jr., at a school in the South Bronx, working under a tough principal who'd completely turned the place around. It was a rough neighborhood, but Mr. Green's school was impeccable. John worked there for about six months, doing street work, connecting with the kids' families, and being a gofer for the CIS staff. He told me that he loved it because nobody knew who he was, or if they knew, they didn't care. The Kennedy name cut no ice in that part of the city.

Before he started work at the school, John came to D.C. for an orientation to CIS. We gave him a place to stay at our house. Jean had gone out for the evening and was appalled when she returned to see that I'd given him single-bed sheets for our double-size sleeper sofa.

"I'm so embarrassed—don't you know what he's used to?" she said to me.

I didn't see what the big deal was. The next morning he didn't act bothered and seemed to have gotten some sleep, wrong sheets or not.

When Bob Baldwin, our board chair, heard that John Kennedy, Jr., was going to be interning with us, he asked me to invite him to Morgan Stanley so that Bob could meet him and share his reminiscences of the Kennedy family. We arrived at Morgan Stanley and the word had obviously gotten out: People were hanging out of their offices and peering around corners, trying to get a look at John. All the women, especially, were dressed up and looking fantastic.

When we were almost at Bob's office, I turned to John and said, "We can't cover everything in the orientation, so here's something I didn't mention—when you travel with me, this happens a lot."

He looked at me, and I could tell that for one awful moment he thought I was serious. Then he cracked up.

Years later, after he'd founded the magazine *George*, we reconnected at a MENTOR fund-raising dinner. I asked John to consider joining our board of directors. He said, "Well, I need to get caught up on what you're doing, so let's schedule lunch."

And within a few weeks, he was gone. It was a stunning, awful loss, for CIS and for all of us.

By 1988, THE CITIES IN SCHOOLS MOVEMENT was reaching tens of thousands of young people at nearly 150 schools in 26 communities. We were getting more requests to start new programs than we could possibly handle. One of our board members, Dan Burke, president and COO of Capital Cities/ABC, insisted that we capture the CIS strategies on paper and set up a training program for new communities.

He called me into his office in Manhattan and said, "Bill, I'm going to teach you two new words: *discipline* and *curriculum*. You and Neil can't keep running all over the country trying to show people how to do CIS. It's inefficient, and by the way, it's killing both of you, in case you hadn't noticed. So you're going to stay put and find a university partner to help you write the curriculum, or else I'm leaving the board and I suggest that you and Neil go find a job."

I said, "Okay, I hear you. I don't mind your going off the board, but the prospect of finding a job—that's scary."

With support from the Department of Justice, we opened the National Center for Partnership Development at Lehigh University in Bethlehem, Pennsylvania, the following year. This training facility operated under the wing of the Iacocca Institute for Competitiveness.

Lee Iacocca, a Lehigh alumnus, had visited one of our Atlanta school sites and agreed to let us be part of this new facility.

As it turned out, "on paper" was wrong. Without realizing the implications, we found ourselves one of the first mainstream educational facilities to benefit from the rising new world of computer technology. Lehigh had created an early prototype of "hypermedia" training for us. The training modules were stored on laser discs, an early forerunner of CDs, and when we loaded a training course onto the computer, we could do amazing stuff like "click on a new link" and "open a new window." Our trainees had to be instructed in the use of a radical device called a mouse. But once everyone got the hang of it, we jumped into the '90s well ahead of the curve. The training program was hugely successful; by 1993, we had more than quadrupled our number of school sites.

Dan Burke took me to meet Lee Iacocca shortly before we began training at Lehigh. The prospect made both of us anxious—me because it was Lee Iacocca, Dan because he was worried that I'd try to explain hypermedia to the titan of American industry.

Naturally, one of Iacocca's first questions was, "Does CIS have any programs in Michigan?"

Fortunately, we did, in Huron County, which is located in the peninsula known as "the Thumb." But I was nervous, and my mind blanked on the exact location.

"Well, um, we've made a small beginning in Detroit," I stammered, "but we've got an operational program in the—in the—you know, in the Finger part of the state."

Iacocca made a face at Dan Burke. "Who is this guy, anyway? He doesn't know the difference between the Thumb," he held up his thumb, "and the Finger." And he held up a finger—you can guess which one.

Fortunately, my confusion about Michigan digits was forgiven, and Iacocca ended up giving us a great endorsement. We made the case that competitiveness was a tough order for a nation with 30 percent of its young people out of the job market because they didn't graduate from high school. Iacocca agreed, saying, "CIS gets results. . . . I am solidly behind it."

My job trying to shape and lead a national organization took me to some strange places, spiritually and emotionally—strange for me, anyway. In my younger days, I was uncompromising, very sure I was right. But getting broken enough and proved wrong enough made me realize that I didn't know as much as I thought.

Some of my '60s friends took offense because I was hanging out with folks from the White House or the financial world. Then again, some of these well-to-do friends were offended by how I hung out with my old "revolutionary" buddies. Once, I was sitting in an airport lounge, dressed in my suit, drinking Starbucks coffee, and talking on my cell phone when I saw a guy I knew from way back in the Pittsburgh days. He was a friend of Joe Bellante's and had known me when we were both street kids. His gaze took me in and then he said, half-joking and half-serious, "Well, Milliken, you finally sold out!"

I couldn't win everyone's approval, and gradually I was learning that I didn't have to. My relationship with the Creator is the first important constant in my life, and my relationship with my family is the other. If those are solid, then I can walk between worlds and do what I can to be about wholeness and community.

The truth is that it's not possible to love kids and also feel contempt for those you're asking to donate money and to volunteer their time. Most people with good fortune and monetary resources want to give back, and they need love, friendship, and community just as much as you or I do, and just as much as a 16-year-old does. I spent too many years being a hypocrite, talking about "loving your neighbor" but secretly believing that those with resources were less caring than I was.

As I began to change that attitude, I started to see how similar we all are in our basic needs. It was part of my constant struggle to stop stereotyping and labeling people. I hated being called a radical, yet I had all kinds of nasty synonyms in my own mind for "wealthy person."

I also watched my attitude change about "being right" in general. In Washington, I could see that ideologues on the left and on the right resembled one another more than they differed. There's the deep-seated anger and the conviction that they alone possess the truth. Watching them helped me become less sure about most things, and that was good. I was no longer positive that I knew how to save the world, although I still charged into every day as though I were earning points. I had to be reminded that it's faithfulness and not success that matters to God.

My little piece of the world, my area of expertise, was kids in danger of being left out and left behind. And as CIS entered more and more schools, I became more willing to speak out about the dropout crisis. We had a national perspective now, and the picture wasn't pretty. Nobody knew exactly how many young people dropped out every year, and the main reason was that nobody *wanted* to know. Educational systems had built-in cover-ups for failure, and one of their best strategies was obfuscating the dropout rate. But by the mid-'80s, I was telling interviewers such as Barbara Thompson at *Christianity Today* that we were probably losing about 30 percent of each graduating class and about 50 percent of the minority students.

It wasn't until the 2006 study by John Bridgeland called *The Silent Epidemic,* commissioned by the Bill & Melinda Gates Foundation, that those numbers were verified. The study found that "almost one-third of all high school students fail to graduate with their class; among minorities, the dropout rate is almost 50 percent." Thanks to the prestige of this study, our message was suddenly taken national, with front-page stories and a *Time* magazine cover devoted to the dropout epidemic.

In the face of such a crisis, what could CIS do? One of the best decisions we made was to expand our idea of what "providing services" to a school meant. When we first brought our work inside the school system, back in Atlanta, we took it for granted that we'd be working with students in the worst shape, the ones with the most problems who were most likely to drop out. For these young people, we coordinated intense social services to keep them in school.

After 20 years, we continued to do this, but we also identified services that could be provided to large groups, even the entire student body, and that had a demonstrable impact on school climate, attendance rates, behavior, and post-graduation options. Drug education programs, career planning, health fairs, mini-courses on making sound economic choices—the list was almost endless, and once again, the community usually had these services in place and ready to go. They just needed someone to coordinate them into the schools.

Increasingly, CIS affiliates began doing this, with excellent results. In large part, this was because we'd succeeded in attracting so many incredibly passionate and talented volunteers and staff. A lot of them were young women and men fresh out of college or graduate school. Others were experienced pros. What they had in common was what I called "magic eyes," which is the consistent ability to see solutions, not problems; possibilities rather than drawbacks; and assets instead of liabilities. Some of these colleagues moved on, while others made a career with CIS, and either way was fine. We wanted to encourage people—young people especially—to follow their calling wherever it took them.

Our role in public school systems also began changing, in a variety of ways. From the first, we encountered resistance from educators who were afraid we were a bunch of arrogant outsiders coming in to make them change. Teachers and principals had every reason to fear this, because all too many school-reform movements took exactly that attitude. Neil Shorthouse used to illustrate this by sketching a school building surrounded by weird, blobby-looking amoebas, saying, "Those are the outsiders, coming to swallow and digest the school." It was like the old joke about relationships: "The two shall become one, and I'm the one!" So we always tried to be sensitive to this, and not come off like we knew better than the professional educators. We wanted to partner with the school system, not take it over.

But then we watched something very interesting happen, in the schools where CIS had the strongest presence. Like a healthy virus, the CIS philosophy started to infect the way the school was run. The principal and staff adopted our approach as their own, emphasizing the critical importance of bringing the community into the school, and integrating services to address children at risk of dropping out, thus freeing up teachers to teach.

"We can't do it alone" was no longer an admission of failure, but rather a rallying cry, an invitation to the community to join the school system in helping all our children succeed. CIS's particular contribution—our "widget," if you will—was the site coordinator, the person who actually worked in the school and coordinated all these efforts. To this day, these folks stand in the breach between the community and the school, serving as the bridge, the healer of the fragmentation that has destroyed so many young lives.

Sometimes CIS got the credit for these innovations, sometimes not. I couldn't have cared less.

OUR DAUGHTER, LANI, ALWAYS RECEIVED a lot of our family's attention and support, and that was possible because her older brother, Sean, was such a great kid. He'd be the first to tell you that growing up with his mother and Lani having constant blowups, and having me gone on business travel much of the time, wasn't easy. He found himself being the mediator and, in some respects, the man of the house. I think children are born with certain personality traits, but circumstances can really bring them out. In Sean's case, even as an infant he was always a pleaser, a rule follower. These characteristics became even stronger as he tried to provide balance in the family for some of the challenges that Lani and I brought.

Sean got through school without much difficulty. He was a natural athlete and played every sport that was available. The Boys Club back in Atlanta was so formative in that regard. It was like a second home for Sean and provided his after-school care. They had unbelievable staff there and treated all the boys like family. The director was a passionate guy who raised funds to get them the best equipment, even though the club was in such a poor section of Atlanta.

Sean has told me that he had no awareness that he was less advantaged than other children (and I've heard this from others who grew up in poor neighborhoods). He never felt unsafe or unhappy. He had a loving environment, a huge extended communal family, and a lot of great adult role models working for social change and caring about their neighbors. He and Lani could walk across Grant Park to school with classmates from the community, then walk to the nearby CIS office after school, or to the Boys and Girls Clubs. And there was no color barrier; Sean felt accepted by everyone he knew, black or white.

When we decided that Sean would go to Woodward Academy for middle school, it was a big change. Woodward wasn't the fanciest private school in the Atlanta area, but it was still an "academy" (not a Street Academy!) with coats and ties, the whole deal. Sean had a long ride home on the same bus that delivered other students all the way to the wealthy north side of Atlanta. The first time he got dropped off in the inner city, there was a visible change in his classmates. They slumped down in their seats, and one kid turned to him and said, "You live *here?* Nobody lives here." If Sean wanted to hang out with anyone from his school, Jean or I had to drive him all over town. And of course the kids at the academy were mostly upper-middle-class white children.

Then we moved to Arlington, Virginia, and Sean had to adjust all over again. He was 14 and just starting high school. But apart from the usual fish-out-of-water issues for the new kid, he did fine. Jean and I always made a point of being there for the important events of his life, no matter what conflicts we might have had. I told him, "I'll always show up for you. I don't care what else is going on in my life." It was a promise I was proud to keep.

Sean went to Virginia Tech, and after graduating spent a few months as a volunteer with Habitat for Humanity. He joined one of their traveling work crews, going all over the Southeast and building houses, sleeping on church floors. He loved it but wasn't sure what direction he wanted his life to take next. I know that he sometimes wished he had parents who would pressure him into a particular career path, but Jean and I always insisted that he make his own choices. And then Sean made two decisions that have made me incredibly happy.

The first was to raise a family with his beautiful wife, Jill. When they got married in 1995, Jean co-officiated at their wedding. She knew that she wouldn't be able to keep it together if she had to stand up there alone and preside over the ceremony. As for me, I didn't even try to be stoic—I was in tears throughout the entire thing. This was the boy we'd almost lost, and I could still feel the anguish of watching him struggle to stay alive in that Atlanta hospital. Then, when Sean and Jill's children, Alexandra and Jack, were born, I felt that my happiness was complete. Ever since I could remember, I'd longed for a family—the bigger the better. Having two great kids like Sean and Lani answered that longing, and now here were two more in the next generation. Incredible!

The other decision Sean made was to follow his call to help his neighbor. He worked for several organizations, including CIS and the Atlanta Boys and Girls Clubs, learning the ropes and coming to a deeper understanding of the challenges facing the nonprofit world. What he realized was this: Perhaps the single biggest headache for a nonprofit, no matter how effective, is creating a consistent, sustainable source of unrestricted funding to build capacity and grow its missions. I'm sure my own complaints about fund-raising for CIS, which he heard at the dinner table year after year while growing up, had a big influence, too. The sources are extremely limited, which means going back to the same donor base every year and asking for a little more money.

Sean saw the huge potential of donated goods and services as a largely untapped resource for nonprofits. Out of this insight, he founded MissionFish in 1999 and soon thereafter brought together a team of like-minded social entrepreneurs and technologists to create an online exchange where nonprofits could accept in-kind gifts, keep anything useful, and sell the rest through auction. The result became a way for nonprofits to turn what they previously viewed as "unkind" gifts—stuff an organization didn't really need or have the capacity to receive, but didn't want to refuse for fear of offending donors—into a new source of unrestricted revenue. In 2003, Mission-Fish partnered with eBay to build eBay Giving Works, which among other great things provides an easy way for eBay users to donate a portion of their sale proceeds to their favorite cause.

Sean and his team expanded MissionFish into the U.K. in 2005, and at this point have raised more than $250 million for nonprofits. Their vision statement is one of the greatest and simplest I've ever heard: "Any cause, any donor, any gift."

So both Sean and Lani have fulfilled my fondest dreams for them. And of course, I'm intensely proud of them. Sean has told me that my optimism, energy, and ability to persevere in the face of great challenges were important values for him to emulate. That means more to me than any other success I could imagine having.

MEANWHILE, CIS CONTINUED TO GROW and was by every measure a national success. Each year, we reached more children, more schools, and more communities. Our programs had been supported in various forms and at various levels by five successive presidential administrations. As happy as I was to see this occurring, my own daily experience was unbelievably stressful. There simply was never enough money to ensure our sustainability, and the fund-raising burden fell largely on my shoulders. The price of success was the awareness of the cost of failure: The stakes were so much higher as our staff grew larger and many more people "downstream"—the CIS state offices, the local communities, and the children themselves—depended on the health of CIS National for their own credibility, and often for their survival.

I felt continually responsible. It seemed that I wouldn't sleep for weeks, which turned into months and years. I knew intellectually that I needed to step back, get healing for myself, and let others share the burden, but the pace and the pressure were so great that I couldn't do it. One crisis followed another, and I believed that I was the only one who could respond effectively.

This unrealistic belief in my own indispensability has been a recurring pattern throughout my life. As I described, Bo Nixon and Clark Jones confronted me about the same issue back in the '60s. I don't think my personality will ever change in this regard, but I get better and better at catching it before I do too much damage to myself and others.

It's all part of the cyclic nature of healing. In 12-step programs, participants speak of always being in recovery, never fully "cured." They also point out how a sober alcoholic can still go on a "dry drunk," falling back into all his old negative behavior patterns, minus the alcohol. Both those observations apply to me and my addiction to responsibility.

So I was part of the problem. I didn't have the administrative skills to take CIS to the next level, and I hadn't put the right leaders in place so that I could step back and do what I do best. I'd describe the challenge as a difference between creative and maintenance leadership. I know how to manage an emerging organization in times of expansion and vision building. But maintenance leadership involves a lot of administrative skills, which I don't have. As long as CIS was largely a creative organization, then Neil and I were perfect for the job. But when it got so much bigger, we also needed the guidance that would stabilize us.

It wasn't a case of "either-or"; it was "both-and." Creativity and vision were still very much required, but someone also had to keep things running on a daily basis—including raising funds—and I was going crazy trying to do it all. There were long periods when coming into the office was like dying every day. The company was deeply in debt. We had too many people in the wrong slots.

Healing is never over, whether we're talking about relationships, the body, or the spirit. Trauma resurfaces from the past, and tragic events add new stress. In the new millennium, my health and that of CIS got better—but first, it all got much worse.

CHAPTER EIGHT

OBJECTS IN MIRROR ARE CLOSER THAN THEY APPEAR

I turned 60 in 2000, and the next decade felt at times as if it would age me another 60 years. There were incredible high spots as Communities In Schools achieved greater and greater national recognition, but also some very rough low points.

Nicholas C. Forstmann became board chair when Bob Baldwin rotated out of that position in 1995. Nick's death from lung cancer at age 54 in February 2001 devastated everyone who knew him. His generosity and kindness were legendary. When Nick knew he was dying, he wrote a short book called *What Really Matters,* addressed to his three young children. He wrote about friendship, work, education, and many other topics. His final thoughts on spirituality made a big impression on me.

Nick was a devout Roman Catholic, and he wrote about how his understanding of religion and the world deepened in the last year of his life: "What is the purpose of congregating for religious study and celebration but to lift spirits and get closer to God, and carry that into your daily life?"

He began working with Dr. Yan Xin, a master of *qigong*, an ancient Chinese healing practice. He wrote, "My definition of the spiritual began to broaden, then. I never knew how to characterize abilities like Dr. Yan Xin's, but surely he was working from some realm most of us don't have ready access to. My thoughts deepened in my walks on the beach. As contact with nature became spiritual, I began to wonder what *wasn't* spiritual."

It appeared that Nick moved from a rather narrow idea of who God is to a more inclusive and open-ended belief, just as I had done. I thanked God that Nick found peace and a deeper love as his death approached. Physical healing isn't the only kind, but that didn't make things any easier for his family and friends.

No sooner had I begun to mourn Nick than it also became clear that his gifts to CIS were irreplaceable. His connections and goodwill in the financial world (he was a founding partner of the investment firm Forstmann Little & Co.) gave us an important source of dollars and partners in Washington, D.C. Each year, he presented our case to members of Congress and helped us secure federal funding that amounted to half our national budget.

After his passing, there was no one to do this. Our new board chair, James M. Allwin, was just finding his feet, taking on responsibilities he hadn't planned for. As the fall of 2001 began, we were anxiously looking around for new fiscal avenues to pursue.

And then the Twin Towers fell.

In an awful way, this felt like a repetition of Nick's death. It was emotionally devastating, and then, just as we were starting to pull ourselves together again, we found out there was a whole new layer of impact. The economy took a big hit in the wake of 9/11, especially the nonprofit world, and we in the CIS network were no exception. To top it off, some of those people in the wrong positions whom I referred to earlier were creating an atmosphere of everyday crisis at CIS National that affected the entire organization.

It was the perfect storm. Everything went wrong at the same time, and each workday began with an ever-more-dire version of the question that had dogged me since we founded CIS: How could we keep the doors open? And what about the hundreds of local and state affiliates who depended on us? We implemented a reorganization that laid off almost one-third of our national staff, and anyone who's gone through that knows how painful it is. But still we were on shaky ground.

Three critical people turned us around. And yes, I'll take some credit for persevering, too, although the stress was almost killing me. First, our longtime board member Jon Powers stepped in to guide our day-to-day operations when we desperately needed his leadership. It wasn't the first time he'd played this role. Jon had left an outstanding career at IBM to lead the United Way of America, stabilizing them after a scandal involving their president. Then, after he joined our board, he served as our interim executive director at a crucial moment in the '90s. We had to call on him to perform this role again, and he generously and selflessly accepted. Having him in the office was the greatest thing that could have happened. Wisely and firmly, he kept us going and guided us toward the next critical decision: the appointment of Dan Cardinali as our president, with me moving to the vice-chairman position.

I wrote quite a bit about Dan in *The Last Dropout*. I knew that I needed to get out of the way and hand over leadership to someone whose skills complemented mine, who could bring stability and direction to our operations and take us to the next level. Dan was that person—and so much more. I wrote in the previous chapter about the distinction between creative and maintenance leadership. We got the best of both worlds in Dan. Not only did he have the ability to run CIS in a way that I never could, but he brought fresh vision, energy, and leadership at every level of the network. Maybe the best way I can say it is this: Had Dan been around in the '70s, I have no doubt that he would have been right there creating CIS with Neil, Dave Lewis, and me.

The third critical person for our turnaround was Nick's successor as board chair. Jim Allwin and Dan quickly agreed on the importance of taking a hard look at CIS's future. The result was a new strategic plan designed after months of study with the help of the well-respected consulting firm The Bridgespan Group. Again, *The Last Dropout* tells more about the specifics of the strategic plan, but the bottom line for me was that I could relax a little. We finally had the leadership we needed, the money was starting to flow again, and our national reputation had survived stronger than ever. Most important, our network of local affiliates had actually continued to grow at a rate of 8 percent a year, despite all the adversity at the national level.

As FOR MY FAMILY LIFE, I FELT more and more joy as I watched my children's success—and my wife's. Jean's journey over the last decade or two has fascinated me. Her spirituality is so strong, and she's matured and broadened in her understanding of God and her calling. Going to seminary was, at the beginning, a way to make sense of her faith in the light of feminism. The church wasn't inclusive of women as leaders. Jean felt that if God created us male and female, then we need both men and women to be leaders so that young people, especially young women, could assert their identities in a healthier way and see God as representative of the whole of humankind.

After we moved to the Washington area, Jean divided her time among the things she loved best: nurturing our marriage, raising our family, and serving in part-time or interim church positions that provided her with counseling opportunities. She also began a part-time private practice in pastoral counseling. Rectors called on her for consultations with their parishioners, and she became more and more focused on couples doing Imago relationship therapy.

Jean has always been ecumenical in spirit, which explains the path she took: Her parents were Roman Catholic and Presbyterian, she went to a Methodist seminary, trained as a counselor in a Baptist hospital, and was ordained an Episcopal priest! She studied psychologist Carl Jung and theologian Paul Tillich to broaden her understanding, especially of the feminine side of God so as to balance all the male emphasis she was raised with in the church. The research paper she wrote to earn her Doctor of Ministry degree at Wesley Theological Seminary explored the use of power and authority by women leading congregations. I've also watched her become involved in interfaith dialogue during her three-and-a-half years as a canon at

Washington National Cathedral. She sees Buddhism, for instance, as a way of practice that comes close to psychotherapy, with its emphasis on detachment, letting go, and centeredness.

Being a pastoral counselor continues the Scripture's wisdom tradition of being a sage, guiding and supporting people as they integrate various understandings of faith. And it's all helped her deepen her commitment to Christ while respecting the ways that others find meaning in their religion. We recently celebrated our 45th wedding anniversary, for which I can only say, "Thank God—it's a miracle!"

Friendships, too, have grown to mean so much to me. Some of the friends of my youth, such as Clark and Edith Jones, Bo Nixon, Reid Carpenter, Joe Bellante, and of course Neil Shorthouse, I've never lost touch with. Clark has been an exceptionally important part of the CIS story, playing so many roles for us throughout the '70s, '80s, and '90s. He eventually became our vice president of operations, overseeing five regional directors, and he and Edith are Lani's godparents. As for Bo, he's right there on the Lower East Side, working the streets. He and his wife, Mary, founded New Life of New York City in 1973, and they're still going strong, helping youth turn their lives around through "relationships, meaningful programs, and the unfailing power of God's love."

Other old friends, I've had to seek out. I remember what a fantastic occasion it was when I visited "Goldbrick" Delaney and his wife, Jerry, after a gap of decades. I'm not sure why I decided to do so, given the time that had passed—I think I must have been in a place where I needed some affirmation. As I described, Goldbrick was the cook at the Young Life camp in Colorado, and the one who stood up for me when I was on the verge of getting kicked out. I wouldn't be sitting here if he hadn't been in my life. Like Thelma, my mother's helper, he was an early African American presence in my life. Thelma is long dead, and that's a regret I have—that I never went back and told her how much she meant to me when I was young and hurting. But Goldbrick was still around. When he retired, he and Jerry bought a little restaurant near Buena Vista, a small community tucked away in the mountains, about an hour from Aspen. I had to be out in Colorado anyway to participate in the Aspen Institute's leadership fellows gathering, so I arranged to stop by.

When I got there, Jerry greeted me and said, "He's not been well, but he knows you're coming. Could you go upstairs to say hi to him?"

Goldbrick was using a cane, and he stood up and burst into tears.

"Come over here," he said. He wrapped me in his arms, and then we were both crying.

"Before I pass on to Jesus, I want to thank you. You and Harv and Vinnie brought the first African Americans out here; the first of my own people."

"No, I have to thank you," I told him. "Do you remember? You stopped me when I was running away. Out in the middle of nowhere—I don't know where I was going. But you brought me back and took me into your and Jerry's little cabin, and then talked Jim Rayburn into letting me stay."

So each of us remembered the other in gratitude, each of us made a difference in the other's life. God has blessed me with a friend like that.

I SOUGHT OUT GOLDBRICK, BUT HEARING from Butch Rodriguez was completely unexpected. He'd left 215 Madison to join the military in 1966, and I knew nothing further about him.

"I hope you are sitting on a comfortable chair," the letter began, "because I believe you will be pleasantly surprised as you continue to read this. I hope that after reading this correspondence, it brings you some fond memories."

It was 2010, and my assistant at CIS had brought this letter in with the day's mail. She'd taken it out of the envelope, or else I didn't bother to look at the return address. Either way, I had no idea who this was from. The writer went on:

> My purpose was to hear your voice once again, and to thank you for the concern, devotion, and dedication you made in rescuing me from the many horrors and destructions that were waiting for me on the streets of the Lower East Side.

This is Anthony "Butch" Rodriguez. Approximately 46 years ago, in 1964, I resided at 215 Madison Street with you and Young Life. I lived among a few other lost and confused souls in dire need of direction. Do you remember? If I am not mistaken, I believe Mr. Dean Borgman was the director of operations during that period.

Later on you sent me to Pittsburgh, PA, during a very difficult period of my life . . . and thereafter I was under the supervision, inspiration, guidance, and direction of another special person in my life, Mr. Reid Carpenter. . . . He supported me, nurtured me, and always gave me a ray of hope in my struggle to find my place in the sun.

Both you and Reid have been my heroes, yesterday, today, and always. Your dedication has always stayed fresh in memory for many, many years. There are several reasons for this correspondence. One is to thank you from the depths of my heart for all of the efforts and assistance you provided in saving me from total self-destruction during my adolescent years.

I hope I did not bore you. It was important to somehow deliver this message to you.

He included his contact info, and I called immediately. Within a minute, we were both laughing and crying over those crazy days on the Lower East Side.

"We had eight guys living in my apartment, remember?" Butch said. "We were the good, the bad, the ugly, and the oogly! But somehow it all gelled. You gave me love and direction and a kick in the butt."

Butch told me that thanks to his experiences at 215 Madison, he was no longer a "functioning moron" when he left us—although he wound up regretting his decision not to enroll at the Blue Elephant and get his diploma.

"What can I say?" he told me. "I'd failed Advanced Sandbox in grade school, so I got my B.S. in Spanglish, a B.S.S. in gutter English, and a Ph.D. in staying alive in the 'hood. I thought those were all the credentials I needed."

After serving a three-year stint in the military, he married and had a child, but the relationship ended after a year and a half. Butch remarried, found a career, and had recently retired. He and his second wife just celebrated 32 years of marriage.

Butch was eager to get back in touch with Reid, too, and that was easy to arrange.

"I just didn't want to disappoint you guys," Butch told me as we said good-bye. I assured him that he hadn't. Far from it—getting his letter was one of the best things that happened to me in 2010.

As I LOOK BACK OVER THE LAST 10 years—the beginning of the 21st century and the decade that ended with my 70th birthday—two moments particularly stand out for me.

The first occurred on November 3, 2007. It was 8 P.M. at the Sheraton Hotel in Atlanta, where more than a thousand representatives of the Communities In Schools national network had gathered to celebrate the organization's 30th anniversary. My book *The Last Dropout*, which told the story of the CIS movement, had just been published, and I was about to embark on a multicity book tour.

I felt as though I was there, but not there at the same time. I thought that I was frozen in my chair, but I found myself walking through a darkened room full of people, weaving through tables of ten to the hot lights flooding the stage. I wanted to speak from my heart to all these friends, colleagues, and family members. I also wanted to be somewhere else—a different place, a different time. It was a bittersweet moment, and I was only starting to understand why. At 67 years old, I was well into the "fourth quarter" of life. Yet all at once, the journey made no sense to me.

How in God's name did I get here? I wondered. *How did I go from street worker to the head of a national organization? Maybe my old Pittsburgh friend at the airport was right—when you get right down to it, am I a sellout?*

It was the final night of our gathering, and I was giving the keynote speech. I thought that I knew what to say, but as I made my way to the podium, the emotions I was feeling were so strong that I was no longer sure.

I reached the stage, squinting against the glare of the lights, waiting for the applause to subside. Back at my table, I could see the most precious people in my life—Jean, Sean, and Lani—smiling at me. I smiled back, and I imagined my grandchildren, Jack and Alex, sitting right there, too. I'd always wanted a family . . . and I finally had one. Yet in a very real way, the entire room felt like family.

It was as if we'd woven something together, using our own lives and gifts as the fabric. Every single person in the room had contributed a strand, a thread, a stitch, a unique contribution without which we wouldn't be able to achieve our mission—which is the "tapestry" we're offering, every day, week, and year to more than a million young people.

The amazing thing was that somehow we'd all learned how to weave the same pattern, to really work together in cooperation and harmony. I always insisted: That's what Communities In Schools is about. It's not a "program." Instead, it's a way to integrate all the resources and caring people in the community and show them how to bring their talents into the schools, where the kids are.

At least I knew where to start my speech. I began calling out the individuals whose love and support mean so much to me, asking the group to thank them with applause. The room resounded with cheers. It gave me a little breathing room—long enough to start to realize what I was feeling.

Most strongly, that was grief, because our board chairman, Jim Allwin, wasn't here. A dear friend for most of the 30 years that Communities In Schools existed, Jim had succumbed to cancer ten days earlier at the age of 54. It was only six years since his predecessor, Nick Forstmann, also a loving friend, had passed away of the same disease at exactly the same age.

I was in Dallas the week Jim died, on my way from one meeting to the next, when I checked my voice mail: *Call this one . . . call that one . . .* and then there was *the* call, the one I knew would be devastating to return. Maria, Jim's wife, wanted me to contact her as soon as possible.

Right then, I knew Jim had left us. The day before, he'd requested last rites, so it was no surprise. But I didn't want to take in that reality. I called Maria, and our talk was as painful as I knew it would be. Yet in the midst of our grief, we also knew that Jim was now free from *his* pain and soaring with the eagles.

Jim Allwin was so much more than a colleague. As I've said, through the worst times, the "perfect storm" when I truly thought we'd have to close our doors, he stood by us and helped us find a way to go on. His service on our board began when he was a 28-year-old protégé of Bob Baldwin at Morgan Stanley. Jim always showed up. In good times and bad, he was the same—focused and steady. So many board members spoke to me about what a calming effect he had on everyone and how secure they felt in his leadership. When he walked in the room, we breathed a collective sigh of relief because we knew that everything would be okay. His positive spirit never denied the difficult realities, but he was confident that we could overcome them. He knew we'd make it.

Jim showed up to help when my son Sean started his own non-profit, MissionFish. He and Maria showed up at a surprise 60th birthday party for me. Maria, who's Greek, rolled up the rugs and had all the kids dancing to bouzouki music. And Jim and Maria were generous and sensitive when they knew our family needed some R & R, making their summer place available to us.

The greatest gift Jim gave me was one he didn't even realize he was giving: He often introduced me as his brother. Standing there at the podium that night in Atlanta, I missed him more than I could say.

Then I felt another realization surface. Looking out at the room, full of people from all walks of life who'd come together around their common love and commitment to children, I understood that I was no longer *caught* between worlds.

All my life, I'd felt stuck in the middle, trying desperately to bring people together so that *I* could feel whole. I went from a comfortable Pittsburgh suburb to the roughest streets of New York City. I tried to speak the truth about poor communities to people born into privilege. I worked to understand how my country could remain divided by racism and the legacy of slavery. I attempted to follow Christ and also oppose the divisiveness of so many churches. So often, I was the one in the middle, not part of one world or the other.

That night, I felt that I'd finally accepted the role God called me to. I realized it was my purpose to be right where I was, making connections and showing others how they might do the same.

So I began my speech.

I talked about the importance of CIS to the school-reform movement. I reminded the audience that if we truly want no child left behind, we have to deal with children coming to school afraid, undernourished, or trying to deal with family crises. Young people have to get turned on to living before they can be turned on to learning.

I talked about how CIS is now a fully professional organization, backing up our love and commitment to children with the most up-to-date, data-driven methods.

Finally, I stated the obvious: The ones we're losing are disproportionately African American and Hispanic. Our country can't go on as a world leader if this continues. Even more important, this is a basic issue of *justice.*

As my speech drew to an end, the emotions I'd felt earlier were suddenly upon me again. My throat began to close as I felt the tears coming. I didn't know what the next words would be.

"Concentrate on love, and miracles happen," I heard myself say. Who was I talking about?

"A guy from Pittsburgh gets to go to Harlem, he gets to meet . . ." My voice trailed off; I couldn't see through the tears.

"This long journey has just been unbelievable." Again I had to stop. Well, these people knew I often got emotional when I spoke. They wouldn't laugh at me.

"We have a great Creator," I started again, "and I'm up here tonight because that Creator gave me a passion. I wasn't a passionate kid. I was hard. But he's softened my heart to where now I can't stand to see one child left behind—let alone one dropping out every eight seconds.

"I have so much to be thankful for. I know it's tough work. But that's what happens when you give your life away: You get it back. There's a generation out there that's longing for a future. We've been gifted with an answer for them. Let's go home and take it to the next level."

The applause began. I finally belonged. This *was* my world. And so I walked back to my table, back to my family.

BUT, TO USE A FAMILIAR PHRASE, GOD wasn't finished with me yet.

The book tour for *The Last Dropout*, which I embarked on after the 30th-anniversary conference, seemed never ending. Every morning, I woke up in a different city, suffering from stomach pain so intense that I couldn't keep any food down. I had a cold that wouldn't go away. I was skipping meals and sleeping even less than usual—three or four hours a night at best.

When I got home, I'd lost 18 pounds, and Jean was frightened. She made me schedule an appointment with our family doctor right away. I knew what she was thinking, and a part of me was afraid of it, too: cancer, just like Jim, just like Nick.

Doctor Hattwick has known me for decades and is part of our house church. His diagnosis was complicated. First, the good news: no cancer. But the bad news was that I'd run down my 67-year-old body as far as it would go. All those years, I'd taken my physical stamina for granted, but that was over now. I could no longer pretend I was a 20-something street worker. The doctor told me that I had infected sinuses and a severe gastric disturbance that would require careful long-term treatment. But mainly, he pointed out the obvious: I was so stressed out that it was a miracle I was still alive.

"You've told me about the hyperactivity, the panic reactions, the 'post-traumatic stress' symptoms," he said. "Are they worse or better when you try to keep going at this pace?"

"A lot worse," I admitted.

"Then you have to take responsibility for your own health, Bill."

Jean was well aware that I'd never really thought of my body as a temple of the Holy Spirit. She told me, "This has to be a turning point. If you don't change, you won't make it. You have a body that has to be cared for."

So with her help and the support of family and friends, I've spent the last three years trying to lead a more balanced life. I made a promise to myself that work wasn't going to be the main show anymore. Family was going to be a priority of equal, if not greater, value.

I've always loved nature and the outdoors, and I'm letting myself spend a lot more time outside, nurturing my spirit. Recently, Jean and I have started meditating, and I can actually sit and do it for 20 minutes—not twice a day yet, but always once a day, which is unbelievable. My stomach only hurts maybe once a month instead of every morning. Thanks to Dan Cardinali and the other great folks at CIS National, I can work only normal hours and feel good about it. An eight-hour day gets me out of the staff's hair and preserves my own sanity, too.

I can't pretend that this change isn't hard on my ego sometimes. I had to confess, for all the world to see, that I didn't have the ability to take Communities In Schools to the next level, to truly take us to scale. That's humbling—and therefore a good thing—but hard to accept. At the same time, I know that I still have an important role to play in CIS's operations and future. I'm no hood ornament, and I never will be.

I always used to tell people that I've never had a job. What I meant was that my calling always led me from circumstance to circumstance, just doing what seemed necessary each step of the way. This means that I don't have anything to retire from, either. I'm committed to young people. That work has taken different shapes over the years, and I could see cutting back even more in years to come, but I'll keep doing it as long as I'm needed.

I'm dwelling on this health stuff for two reasons: first, I want to emphasize that the healing journey is *never* finished. There I was at 67, making the same mistakes I'd made since I was a street worker in Harlem—driving myself too hard and not acknowledging the need for more inner healing.

It reminds me of that sticker you see on a lot of car side mirrors: "Objects in mirror are closer than they appear." All my hurting places, limitations, and shames aren't just distant memories. They're still with me, still clearly visible. I've returned to Henri Nouwen's words: "Finding the treasure is only the beginning of the search." This time, though, I think I may finally have gotten the message.

The second reason I'm talking about my health challenges is to keep other young entrepreneurs from making the same mistakes I did. I thought that I was invincible, but every time I stretched myself past the healthy limit, mentally and physically, I only ended up frustrating my colleagues and hurting myself.

AND THEN IT WAS 2010, AND EVERYONE started going anniversary crazy. It was my 70th birthday, and also the 50th anniversary of that June morning when Vinnie and I first walked onto a Harlem basketball court looking for a game.

I hadn't foreseen it, but I overheard some board members plotting after a meeting and realized that a lot of people were anxious to mark the occasions. It would be good publicity for Communities In Schools, and I was all in favor of that. But the more plans that the board and my colleagues made for parties and commemorations (and PR materials), the less I could relate to it. It was starting to feel like a big hassle, something I had to get through.

Vinnie was long gone, dead from a heart attack in his 30s. He'd gotten his degree, married, and gone on to work with kids through the YMCA. He died playing basketball, doing what he loved best: hanging out with young people and giving them hope for the future.

Bo Nixon was very much with us, however, and we decided to feature him in a film that Albert Maysles was making about Communities In Schools, to coincide with the anniversary of my 50 years working with kids. *Never Give Up on a Child* (which you can watch at **www.vimeo.com/18471748**) would show a number of wonderful CIS affiliates around the country and some great student success stories. The filmmakers wanted to bookend these vignettes by showing Bo and me on a trip back to our old hangouts on the Lower East Side.

I agreed, wondering what the experience would be like. Being followed around by cameras sounded pretty awful. But as it turned out, Maysles and the crew were such excellent filmmakers that after a while, Bo and I forgot they were there. Nothing was posed or rehearsed—they just trailed us as we walked through the old neighborhood, noticing all the changes and reminiscing about people we'd known.

A few pages back, I said that there were two key moments from the last ten years that seem to stand for something important about where my life has journeyed. The first was that speech in Atlanta during the aftermath of Jim Allwin's death.

The second came as Bo and I were walking across the Alfred E. Smith Housing Projects, where so many of the kids I first knew in New York were raised. The camera crew followed us, recording our visit for the film.

Just then, a shout came from across the square: "Bobo! How's my brother!"

A guy trotted up to us, greeted Bo warmly, and began pulling a lot of papers out of a manila envelope. He was so excited that he obviously had no time for small talk.

"Look at this! We got a baby going to the University of Texas school of nursing. I've got all the papers right here. I'm so proud of my daughter!"

By that point, he looked and sounded familiar, but I couldn't quite place him.

"Thank God for people like you," he said to Bo. "You saved my life. My 'Young Life,'" he added, smiling. Okay, he was someone from the Young Life days.

Then Bo asked casually, "Remember Bill?"

The guy took a good look at me, and I thought he was going to start doing somersaults, he was so flipped out.

"Milliken! Oh my God! Lord have mercy! Bill Milliken! I used to work for you!" He gave me a gigantic hug. "I was a junior counselor—am I right or wrong?"

Then I knew him—it was a guy named Randy Santiago. "You're right," I said, laughing. Then came another hug.

"I haven't seen you in, what—35 years?" It had been closer to 45, but I didn't correct him. "I remember you, brother! Peace and love, my brother!"

As we walked away, he was still grinning at us, waving his manila envelope.

Bo and I got into the car to leave, but I kept looking back.

"I can't believe his daughter is in nursing school," said Bo.

"I know," I agreed . . . and I finally had a moment that felt real to me, in the middle of all the hassles and complications surrounding the anniversary.

Bo and I had started something that was still going. Fifty years later, Randy Santiago's daughter was off to nursing school. That's the power of love in action. It's unconditional and unstoppable, a force that changes lives, families, and entire communities.

That's an incredible sight to see in the rearview mirror—and the journey is far from over.

EPILOGUE

A Letter to My Great-Grandchildren

Dear Ones:

So how's life in 2060?

When you read this, I'll be long gone—at least I hope so! The idea of living to be 120 years old has no appeal for me. Maybe your generation has seen an amazing increase in human longevity, and 120 is the new 80. That would be great, but I'm perfectly happy to have made it to 70.

Yes, I'm sure there are a lot of fantastic things you could tell me about. New inventions, exciting art and music, and discoveries that have changed the way you live.

Do I dare to hope that you have a cure for cancer now, and that there's abundant clean water for everyone on the planet? Is it possible that nations are starting to find a way besides war to resolve their differences? In our own nation, is the discourse more civil, more focused on what we have in common rather than on what divides us?

That would all be a dream come true. But the question I really want to ask is this: Are you more connected, more truly alive in the spirit, than we are now?

In my lifetime, we've learned a new word: *connectivity.* All at once, everyone has access to the technology that can create a global village, but a strange thing has happened. People, especially young people, have a lot more connectivity . . . but a lot less connection. We invented social networking, and some of us have forgotten why one-on-one personal relationships matter. All the "informationships" in the world are not a substitute for truly human connections.

As for the adults, we continue to fight our battles, both physical and political. All that connectivity hasn't helped us find peace yet. Our children are still paying the price, growing up in poverty and despair in the world's richest nation.

That's another question I'd like to ask you: Has the United States finally united around children? In 2060, perhaps no child is left behind—for real.

As I said in my opening letter to your parents (and please give them my best and be nice to them, now that they're almost my age), I wouldn't have bothered writing this book if I thought it was just my memoir. I wanted to spend a good part of my 70th year looking back at the journey that brought me here, because I believe there are lessons and experiences that I can pass on to others, particularly a younger generation that seems intensely interested in social justice.

There's a song I really like by the group Pink Floyd. It's called "Another Brick in the Wall." Whenever I hear it, I'm reminded of the choice we face each day. In our small, seemingly unimportant interactions with people—strangers, colleagues, and loved ones—our behavior can put up one more brick in the wall that divides us, or it can take one down, letting in a little more light and a little more room to reach out.

Not since my own youth in the 1960s have I met so many young men and women who are on fire with the call to give back, to help others, and to take down the walls, brick by brick. As I write this, I'm wondering whether you, too—children of my granddaughter, Alex, and my grandson, Jack—are part of a generation that can benefit from the lessons of one person's often-painful journey. I began on the streets of Harlem in 1960—exactly 100 years ago as you read this, but maybe it's still relevant.

I've lived life fully and passionately—made lots of mistakes and experienced big failures, but learned from both. I've been blessed with lots of people who prayed and cared for me and helped me through my own "valley of the shadows." I found that life is often difficult and painful, but also incredibly good, and that out of suffering, hope and healing may be born. I've learned that love is stronger than hate and that people hunger for community and want to give back. Truly, it's relationships that change people, not programs. As many times as I've wanted to quit, I've never given up, just as the people who loved me never forsook me.

I don't want you to think I'm a theologian. I'm just sharing what I've learned from my own life experiences, not from reading books. You can decide for yourself if any of it applies to you. So here, as briefly as I can, are the insights I hope this book might provide for you and others:

• *Life is about relationships and grace.* We're offered these precious opportunities—the grace—to heal our own wounds in our interactions with others. We don't move forward because of what we "deserve" or how hard we work to get divine love. It's not about abiding by rules. We're not going to *earn* anything spiritually. I thought that I could prove myself worthy, in my own eyes and in God's, by working too hard and ignoring my own needs. But we can't summon grace that way.

We're all in the same boat, equally and thoroughly messed up, full of flaws, sins, and self-doubt. We develop certain skills in order to cover up our deficiencies—or at least that's how it feels at the time. And then it turns out those skills are exactly what God wants for us. I saw that everyone, especially young people, wants to be listened to and empathized with. So I decided to become good at that because I secretly believed it was all I *could* be good at, because I was dumb. Yet all along, following this path prepared me for the job God called me to do. That's grace in action.

This may sound almost like an abdication of responsibility, but in fact it's harder to live with grace than with guilt. If I'm forgiven, then I don't have any excuses. I can't blame my own brokenness for my failures to do what God calls me to do.

We all have our own "shadows"—our hurts, resentments, and secret dark side. It's only grace that allows us to move on in the Spirit. God's grace was responsible for most of my successes, yet only now can I see the patterns, which weren't visible to me at the time. I've learned to accept this as divine synchronicity—the presence of God, shaping my life and the lives of others.

You're about the same age that I was when I was working on the streets of New York City, struggling to overcome the challenges I saw around me, and unconsciously struggling for my own wholeness. Maybe you, too, are feeling confused by your challenges and are unable to see the synchronicity. Of course, I hope you've already figured out how God is working in your lives. But if not, just knowing that the patterns are there and that you *will* see them eventually may help make everything a bit easier. So often it can look as though your world is falling apart, when in fact the pieces are coming together—if you could only see it in the rearview mirror.

I thought no one cared, I thought I was dumb, and I was afraid of failure. Maybe you share some of those fears. . . . Welcome to the human race. You have to trust God to call you to the right spots and give you the proper skills and community.

• *Out of brokenness come empathy, compassion, forgiveness, and the possibility of healing.* Experiencing your own flaws is the first step on the journey to hope, healing, and then helping others. Intense hurt is often necessary for any kind of growth. You're my family, and I don't want to see you suffering, but no one gets through life by looking good and feeling no pain. When we're in pain, God is giving us the opportunity to grow.

The amazing thing is that what I thought was an outward journey, a call to work with others, was also an inward quest to find the person I was created to be. The two paths are one and the same, like breathing in and breathing out. There's my own fragmentation: How do I put myself back together and be a whole person? And there's the fragmentation of society: How can I work for justice and be committed to kids? Each question has allowed me to see deeper into the other; in a mysterious way, they're part of the same inquiry. At first, I thought I was in New York City to "help people." But ever since my first days in Harlem, I couldn't ignore the fact that I was the one who needed help—and hope and healing.

• *Therefore, the outward journey and the inward journey are always connected.* Being hurt and broken opens us to the pain of others, so we're motivated to help. But if we skip our own healing, we wind up working out our issues on other people. I think all of us do "street work," whatever form it may take, in part to escape ourselves, as well as to try to follow our calling. The things we're always judging and criticizing in others are usually the hidden fears and weaknesses in ourselves. Too often (and I've tried to be honest about it in this book) I've ignored my inward journey and the result was unhealthy physically, emotionally, and spiritually.

From my street work to my love for my own family, I've seen this truth played out over and over: What we do for others, we do for ourselves. I wanted to help homeless, drug-addicted kids find a community that could turn their lives around—and that was exactly what *I* needed, too. I made a commitment to help my daughter— your great-aunt Lani—find understanding and self-acceptance, and in the process she helped *me* to do the same.

This is an area where my mode of relational thinking has really aided my understanding, because the process isn't linear at all. Healing is a spiral, a cycle that's constantly repeating at different levels. In 12-step programs, participants speak of people always being "in recovery," never fully cured. That seems exactly right to me. This cycle of growth toward wholeness—going in, going out, and constantly finding new levels of God's grace—has never stopped in my life, and I'm sure it never will.

I can only imagine and pray that this will be true for you, too: You get your life by giving it away.

• *Spiritual principles are practical.* They're designed to help you lead a healthy, whole, giving life, not to become a law-abiding "religious person." Simply following the rules won't get you into heaven. Sermons, proselytizing, and guilt-trips aren't going to open anyone up to the Spirit.

If I don't steal, it's because I can't love my neighbor and steal from her, not because it's the law. The beatitudes and other Gospel truths aren't a collection of lofty ideals that we can't live up to. We learn their truth through the lessons of our own lives. When principles are truly flexible and based on spiritual understanding, they free us instead of trapping us in legalistic structures.

I've noted at several points in this book that there's a strong tendency for well-meaning believers to wind up worshipping their church, temple, or mosque instead of God. The Gospel goes in the other direction. It's about grace and inclusion, not sectarianism.

I've had to change a lot of my attitudes about institutional religion. For all the ways I failed academically, one thing I can say for myself is that I always questioned everything. I went from a fairly strict Christian belief to a much more aggressive attitude about churches and their hypocrisies, and finally came to an acceptance of the role of organized worship in my life.

My position now is simple: Don't throw out Christianity, Judaism, Hinduism, or Islam—or God in any form—because of the hypocrisy of believers. We all fall short, so join the crowd! There are no perfect systems or people. We work out our own salvation with fear and trembling. It's easier to say who's in and who's out, the way some dogmas do, than to accept that we all have our own shadows; we're all saints and sinners at the same time.

To me, a good worship community is a place where we can be honest about this basic fact. Your parents grew up with a deep faith, thanks to the spiritual values and gifts that were passed down to them from *their* parents, so I'm betting the pattern has continued, and you've found an honest, nurturing faith community, too.

My relationship with our Creator is the first important constant in my life, and my relationship with my family is the other. If those are solid, then I can go out in the world and do what I can to be about wholeness and community.

• *Everybody needs connection—but what kind?* No program in the world is going to help a young person find his or her future, and technology won't replace personal relationships.

Nearly everything I've learned about relating to people one-on-one grew out of my commitment to youth and the desire to give them hope and a future. But I've come to understand that if it's true for a kid, it's probably true for everyone. We have to be honest with young people and expect honesty from them . . . and then realize that this applies to adults as well. The only surefire destroyer of community is lying. We also have to give people their freedom, and that sometimes means living with the consequences of their choices. We have to let go and let God be in charge. Continuing to "help" isn't always beneficial.

If you look in your Multi-Maxi-Kindle, or whatever your reading device is called in 2060 (it's probably implanted in your brain by now, instead of being one of those clumsy handheld devices, right?), you might be able to find a book I wrote in 2007 called *The Last Dropout*. In it, I tell a story about being on a panel at a government hearing where someone asked me, "What's the difference between the kids you've seen make it and the ones who haven't?" I told him, "The ones who made it did so because we *allowed* them to make it. The greatest gift you can give someone is to allow them to give something to *you*." This is as essential as developing a generous spirit in yourself. There comes a point where the helping has to stop. We have to decide if we really mean it when we say, "It's more blessed to give than to receive."

I also spent years learning to distinguish between the positive and negative uses of anger. No one can be on the cutting edge of justice without feeling angry. But it took me a long time to figure out how to use that as a way to connect with people and inspire them rather than just rant at them. It's the difference between personal upset, born out of hurt, and a passionate, prophetic rage that can speak for all of us. I was around your age when I first had to learn to make this distinction, so maybe what I've written about it will be useful to you, too.

• *Standing in the breach and trying to connect the dots is really about a longing to integrate worlds.* That's the only way to be part of all of them. It's a desire for wholeness and community. Being the one in the middle can be painful, but it's something everyone does at least some of the time. Everyone's life has fragmented, apparently irreconcilable elements. At some point, it seems as if most people face the challenge of being an integrator. For me, the journey has been one of acceptance. It's the difference between feeling torn apart and burdened, and arriving at a place where being in the middle feels like a calling and a gift.

These opportunities come up all the time. When you go to your job and then come home to be with your family, you're making connections; you're a living bridge between two worlds. How well will you integrate them? You'll never do it perfectly, but with grace you'll come to accept this as part of your identity and wholeness.

Of course, all this has a wider social implication as well. The American experience I've lived through has been a constant call for someone to stand in the breach, especially around issues of race and economic justice. As a result, a lot of racial barriers are down now, compared with when I was a young man in the mid-20th century. I suppose you learned this in your history classes, but it may still be hard to believe: All across the American South, a person of color couldn't ride in the front of a public bus or drink from the same water fountain as a white person. In my lifetime, that changed. There's much less overt discrimination now, and there are more positive images and role models for minority youth. We created a national holiday to celebrate Dr. Martin Luther King, Jr., the greatest leader of my generation and a martyr for the civil-rights movement.

But now that there's more real equality of interaction between races, different tensions have come up. Even today, there are only so many places for people of color to succeed, and only so many individuals can fill those places. The filter is bigger, but it's still there. The structure still favors those who have power and resources, and structural racism is more powerful than individual prejudice. The de facto quota system will only tolerate so many of "them."

Racism in the 20th century was overt—everyone knew what it looked like. Today, though, bigots know better than to sound bigoted. They find different issues to use. For instance, anti-immigration and anti-terrorism efforts, and xenophobia in general, are all new faces of racism. I hope you've inherited a society that's overcome much of this, but I have a feeling that the struggle is still going on in 2060—that some group is still being denied justice and equality.

Where I'm sitting in 2012, we don't have to look far to see the same old crap: an African American can commute on a train every week for years, but the seat next to him is never taken, and people of color always seem to get grouped together in public venues. For all the incredible changes—including the election of our current President, Barack Obama, whom I'm sure your history classes celebrate as the first African American to lead our country—we're not "post-racial America" yet. We still need people willing to stand up against classism, economic injustice, sexism, homophobia, and racism of all types, whether it's targeting African Americans, Latinos, Asians, or any other group of supposed outsiders.

At the moment, it looks as though poverty is, and will remain, the great justice issue in 21st-century America. We have one of the highest poverty rates of any industrialized nation, and income disparity grows worse every year. Anyone born into poverty has the odds strongly stacked against him or her. Has the America of 2060 begun to close the gap between the haves and the have-nots? For your sake, I hope so. No country can survive and prosper with one-fifth of its people in poverty, which is the case in the U.S. today.

So there remains a great need for action and great challenges to be met. Not everyone can do everything, nor is everyone called to a public role, but we all can do *something*. Quincy Jones's metaphor of an orchestra, where each member plays a different instrument, remains the key illustration for me. We need to work together and value each other's diverse gifts and skills.

NOW BE HONEST: HAVE YOU READ this entire book, or did you do what I would have done and skipped to the end, to this letter addressed to you? If so, please go back and read the whole thing. Your Great-Grandpops worked very hard on it, and you'll find out who Quincy Jones is and why his orchestra metaphor is so great!

I believe there's something incredibly important about seeing children as a rallying point, a reason to make connections and close the gaps between us. Our society is so badly divided today. But no one, regardless of their politics, thinks kids should pay the price of our dysfunction. They're truly blameless. When I've spoken to wealthy corporate leaders about the things that all children need and want—safety, health, and education—I always see them relating it to their own little ones. There's no division or disagreement. We may yet bring our country—and our world—together by focusing on the plight of young people.

Has it happened for your generation? Is the year 2060 a time when the United States is united around children? Does every kid have an equal chance for success, happiness, and love?

From way back here, all I can say is, "God bless you. May all your dreams come true."

Much love,
Great-Grandpops

ACKNOWLEDGMENTS

Writing a memoir may sound like a solo task, but that's far from the truth. My ideas and recollections have been nurtured throughout the process by so many gifted, dedicated people. Three in particular deserve my heartfelt thanks.

My dear wife, **Jean Milliken**, read this book in draft after draft, checking facts, prompting memories, and offering her own invaluable insights. I can only imagine her initial reaction when I told her that I wanted to try to tell the story of our life together! But she was there for me every step of the way, and I couldn't have done it without her.

John Morris has been not only a valued friend and gifted writer for more than 20 years, but also a fellow seeker on his own spiritual journey. This book would never have been possible without his keen mind, deep faith, unflagging commitment, and consistent eloquence.

Sally DeLuca kept watch over our work, participated with unfailing wit and intelligence in dozens of "Monday book meetings," and contributed editorial improvements of the highest caliber. More than this, she was a model of patience and clarity, never losing sight of the goal and always helping me organize my thoughts to find the right path.

Beyond these three essential collaborators, I want to gratefully acknowledge the contributions of **Neil Shorthouse** and **Dan Cardinali,** whose friendship and guidance have meant so much to me; **Gerry Breslauer,** an incredible friend and CIS board member, who insisted I write this book and should get all the blame; **Jillian Manus,** agent extraordinaire, great friend, and great board member; **Jessica Kelley** from Hay House, who made this a much better book with her sharp editing; and **Marjory Zoet Bankson, Peter Bankson, Katie Fisher,** and **Leigh Somerville,** who all gave generous and perceptive reactions to the manuscript in its various stages.

Finally, this book would have been dull indeed without the recollections of my old friends, colleagues, and family members who agreed to be interviewed and quoted: **Robert H. B. Baldwin, Joe Bellante, Reid Carpenter, George Johnson, Clark Jones, Keith Miller, Bob Milliken, Sean Milliken, Robert "Bo" Nixon, Dean Overman, Butch Rodriguez,** and **Onita Terrell.** To each of you, I send a huge thank-you for being part of my life, and part of this story.

ABOUT THE AUTHOR

Bill Milliken has been a tireless advocate for disenfranchised youth and one of the foremost pioneers in the movement to connect schools with community resources to help troubled students graduate and succeed in life. In 1977, he and others developed a model organization, now known as Communities In Schools, which he served for more than 25 years as national president and currently as vice chairman of the board. Bill has advised U.S. Presidents of both political parties and has received numerous awards, including the Edward A. Smith Award for Excellence in Nonprofit Leadership, the Champion for Children Award from the American Association of School Administrators, the National Caring Award from the Caring Institute, the Temple Award for Creative Altruism from the Institute of Noetic Sciences, the national Jefferson Award for Public Service, and an honorary doctorate from Bard College. He is the author of *Tough Love; So Long, Sweet Jesus;* and *The Last Dropout.*

Contact: **founder@cisnet.org**

NOTES

NOTES

NOTES

NOTES

NOTES

NOTES

NOTES

NOTES

NOTES

NOTES

NOTES

NOTES

Hay House Titles of Related Interest

YOU CAN HEAL YOUR LIFE, the movie, starring Louise L. Hay & Friends
(available as a 1-DVD program and an expanded 2-DVD set)
Watch the trailer at: **www.LouiseHayMovie.com**

THE SHIFT, the movie,
starring Dr. Wayne W. Dyer
(available as a 1-DVD program and an expanded 2-DVD set)
Watch the trailer at: **www.DyerMovie.com**

FRIED: Why You Burn Out and How to Revive, by Joan Borysenko, Ph.D.

THE GIFT OF FIRE: How I Made Adversity Work for Me,
by Dan Caro, with Steve Erwin

*A MINDFUL NATION: How a Simple Practice Can Help Us Reduce Stress,
Improve Performance, and Recapture the American Spirit,* by Tim Ryan

THE POWER OF YOUR SPIRIT: A Guide to Joyful Living, by Sonia Choquette

*UNBINDING THE HEART: A Dose of Greek Wisdom, Generosity, and
Unconditional Love,* by Agapi Stassinopoulos

All of the above are available at your local bookstore,
or may be ordered by contacting Hay House (see next page).

We hope you enjoyed this Hay House book. If you'd
like to receive our online catalog featuring additional information
on Hay House books and products, or if you'd like to find out
more about the Hay Foundation, please contact:

Hay House, Inc., P.O. Box 5100, Carlsbad, CA 92018-5100
(760) 431-7695 or (800) 654-5126
(760) 431-6948 (fax) or (800) 650-5115 (fax)
www.hayhouse.com® • **www.hayfoundation.org**

Published and distributed in Australia by: Hay House Australia Pty. Ltd.,
18/36 Ralph St., Alexandria NSW 2015 • *Phone:* 612-9669-4299
Fax: 612-9669-4144 • www.hayhouse.com.au

Published and distributed in the United Kingdom by: Hay House UK, Ltd.,
292B Kensal Rd., London W10 5BE • *Phone:* 44-20-8962-1230
Fax: 44-20-8962-1239 • www.hayhouse.co.uk

Published and distributed in the Republic of South Africa by:
Hay House SA (Pty), Ltd., P.O. Box 990, Witkoppen 2068
Phone/Fax: 27-11-467-8904 • www.hayhouse.co.za

Published in India by: Hay House Publishers India, Muskaan Complex,
Plot No. 3, B-2, Vasant Kunj, New Delhi 110 070 • *Phone:* 91-11-4176-1620
Fax: 91-11-4176-1630 • www.hayhouse.co.in

Distributed in Canada by: Raincoast, 9050 Shaughnessy St., Vancouver, B.C.
V6P 6E5 • *Phone:* (604) 323-7100 • *Fax:* (604) 323-2600 • www.raincoast.com

Take Your Soul on a Vacation

Visit **www.HealYourLife.com®** to regroup, recharge,
and reconnect with your own magnificence.
Featuring blogs, mind-body-spirit news, and life-changing
wisdom from Louise Hay and friends.

Visit **www.HealYourLife.com** today!

Harlem Streets, 1981, oil painting on canvas by LeRoy Neiman.
Donated by the artist to Communities In Schools and used with permission.